# Insider Secrets: Mastering Search on Ancestry.com

### 50 Tutorials & Tips for
### Beginning, Intermediate, & Advanced Users

Jim Mosher

# Preface

Ancestry is the most used genealogical research site in the world. With over 19 billion records and 80 million family trees, it has become the go-to site for many family historians. Knowing that there are 19+ billion records is one thing. Knowing how to find the person you are looking for is something else. This guide – written by a former Ancestry Search Product Manager – will give you the inside edge on making discoveries on Ancestry.

Whether you are just starting your journey or have been around the block a few times, there are tips and tricks that will help you. From doing a simple search to understanding why Ancestry gives you the results it does, this book will help you understand not just the *how* but also the *why* as you explore the vast Ancestry.com collections.

# TABLE OF CONTENTS

# PART 1: AN INTRODUCTION TO ANCESTRY

# GETTING STARTED WITH FAMILY HISTORY

As you start your journey of discovery for your family history, you often start from a story or recollection:

- Everyone says I look just like my grandfather...
- My family all came to America during the Potato Famine...
- Mom always said we had Native American heritage...
- I have a picture of my Great Aunt Sarah...
- I remember a cabin in the woods from a childhood vacation...

These, and other memories, spark a desire to learn more about the people who came before you. Who are they? Where did they live? What did they do? What were they like? Am I anything like them? Is my love for hiking or swimming or reading or dancing or playing cards attributable to my heritage?

When you come to Ancestry – and most other family history sites – you come looking for a person or a family. However, Ancestry doesn't have people or families. Ancestry has records (such as documents, certificates, lists, and books). These records provide *evidence* about a person – where they were born, where they lived, who they loved. Your goal is to discover what you can about your family from these records and from the times and places they lived.

Allow me to share a personal example. My mother's father passed away when she was quite young. She has few memories of him or his family. I wanted to find out more about him and his heritage. As I explored, I discovered Henry, my maternal great-great grandfather (my mother's great grandfather). Henry was born in Ohio in 1868, three years after the Civil War. He married at age 20, and, over the next 11 years, he and his wife had five children. He worked as a blacksmith and then, later in life, as a mechanic. Sadly, his wife passed away shortly after their youngest was born, just after the turn of the century.

Henry, proud father of five, had to be concerned. How could he work and take care of an infant and several children not yet old enough to care for themselves? The answer is complicated. Henry did marry again, and relatively quickly. (Henry was engaged within six months of his wife's passing. That engagement ended in August. Henry was married to another young lady in September.) However, for those six months, the children had to be under someone's care. Many were taken in by other families. One ended up in an institution. It is possible that Henry and his new bride cared for some of the children for a while, but the records show that they lived alone during at least a portion of the children's formative years.

How did I discover all of this? Was there a full history of Henry on Ancestry, just waiting for me to read? Did the amazing professional genealogists who work for Ancestry compile this information on my behalf? Did my search for Henry provide me with a personal account of his life?

No. I pieced the details of Henry's life together from the *records* available on Ancestry. I discovered pieces and parts of his history on documents that cataloged where he lived as well as who he was with. I explored the lives of his children and wives to gain insight into the overall family life. From these varied sources, I put together a picture of Henry that I could share with my mother. This is a picture of a hardworking man who loved his wife deeply and who wanted what was best for his children – even if that meant letting others help raise them while he provided financial support. He had a hard life. However, his children, for the most part, had a much better life due to his sacrifices. That is a heritage my mother could relate to, as she recalled the stories of her father as recounted by her mother.

Those stories are why we do family history. Finding those details so we can document and remember the lives of those who came before us is incredibly important. It helps us understand our heritage and the legacy left by those who came before.

Will you be able to tell every story? Unfortunately, no. Some lives are too sparsely documented in the historical and private records. However, as you make connections, you will discover key pieces of your history, and the over-arching storyline that leads to *you* will become clearer.

My goal in creating this guide is to help you along that path. Using this guide, you will learn how to find the records that hold the details to these stories. If you are new to Ancestry, you will learn how to get started. If you have been at this for a while, there are some tips and tricks that may help you dig a bit deeper to find some elusive details. And, for those who just need a refresher, there is a summarized list of tips and tricks at the back.

# YOUR SEARCH STRATEGY – THREE SIMPLE GUIDELINES

Ancestry doesn't have information about people. It does have records that describe people. Some of the records are part of the governmental record-keeping process – census lists, voter registration, military service, birth and marriage documents, death certificates, travel documents, and others. Some are records created by other family history enthusiasts such as yourself, assembling their view of their family history through the Ancestry Member Tree system. Purists will argue that the public trees on Ancestry are not records. I will assert that they are. They are simply a different kind of record that may put you on the path to discovery.

Knowing that Ancestry has records about people, you must shift your mindset when searching. Do not search for a person. Search for facts *about* a person. Those facts will help you tell the story or make a connection to another generation.

What does this mean, in practice?

- **Start with what you know about a person**. You may have a name and a place. You may know the names of children or a spouse. You might have a cemetery photo. You have some details about this person, or you wouldn't be looking for more information about them.
- **Identify what you want to know**. You may not know when your ancestor was married, or where she lived during the Great Depression, or where she is buried, or the name of her sister's husband. Once you know *what* you are looking for, it is much easier to find it.
- **Search in the right places to fill in the gaps**. Ancestry has a huge hay stack, and you are looking for a particular needle. By narrowing down what you want to find, and by determining where best to find it, you will be more efficient in your searches. And the more efficient you are, the more exciting discoveries you can make.

# WHAT ABOUT HINTS?

If you document your family history in a family tree on Ancestry, then you can take advantage of the famous Ancestry Shaky Leaf. These leaves represent searches done for you in the background, matching the information you provide about a person to the records in the Ancestry data set. By exploring these hints, you may discover many of the most important milestone records in your ancestor's life – when they were born, where they lived, who they married, and when they died.

But not everyone has a tree on Ancestry. And hints only cover part of the Ancestry collection. Knowing how to search effectively will help you find more records and fill in more details about your family.

Should you use hints? Absolutely. They are a great resource. But you must remember that they are a hint. A computer matched things up. And it often does a great job. But the computer is not infallible. As Agatha Christie's famous detective Hercule Poirot was fond of saying, you must use "the little grey cells" when evaluating a hint, just as they must be used when evaluating search results. Just because information is provided to you as a hint or a search result *doesn't mean that the information applies to your ancestor.* Use the little grey cells.

# GETTING STARTED WITH SEARCH

For those who are relatively new to Ancestry, this section should help understanding:

- How to find the search forms on Ancestry
- How to do some basic searches
- How to interpret the search results

You will be led, step by step, through a search. You will be introduced to key terms that are used through the rest of the book.

If you are completely comfortable with the basics of searching on Ancestry, feel free to skip over this section. But if you find I am using terms that you are unfamiliar with, you may want to come back to this section for a quick review.

Please note that this book is not a full tutorial on using Ancestry. It does not cover how use the Tree system, although the Trees are referenced. You won't find details on DNA research. It is, however, a great way to learn how to search effectively on Ancestry.

## YOUR FIRST SEARCH ON ANCESTRY

For this example, we are going to look for information about George W Scott's parents. We know George was born in Missouri around 1890, and we know he was married to Oma L (maiden name unknown). He lived in Missouri in 1930. We don't yet know who his parents are. Parents are typically listed on Census records, if we can find George living with his parents. Parents might be listed on a marriage record as well; if we can get a clue from a marriage record, we might be able to figure out which George W Scott is *our* George W Scott.

(See what we did there? We identified what we know and what we want to know. This helps us choose how we might search and what records to look for.)

Search is available from the *Header* on Ancestry. To get to the Search options, click the **Search** link in the header.

The Search menu provides several entry points into search. At the top, *All Collections* lets you search all of the content on Ancestry. At the bottom, the **Card Catalog** lets you explore what individual collections Ancestry has available; the **Member Directory** lets you search for other Ancestry members. Everything in between are *search categories*. You can search the Census collections on Ancestry. Or you could search just the Immigration & Travel collections.

For this example, let's choose **All Collections**. Normally, I would look in the Census category and correlate what I find there with results from the **Birth, Marriage, & Death** category, but we'll keep this first one simple.

The *Global Search* form lets you search all collections. If there is a link on your search form that says **Show more options**, click it. That will give you the full power of the Global Search form. (If the link says **Show fewer options**, you are already at the right place.)

| First & Middle Name(s) | Last Name |
|---|---|
| | |
| **Place your ancestor might have lived** | **Birth Year** |
| City, County, State, Country | |

SEARCH   Show more options ⌄ ← If you see this, click it to expand the search form.

You will enter your *search criteria* into the form. The search criteria reflect the information you know about a person. You use what you know to find out things you don't know.

Let's take a moment to look at the Global Search form:

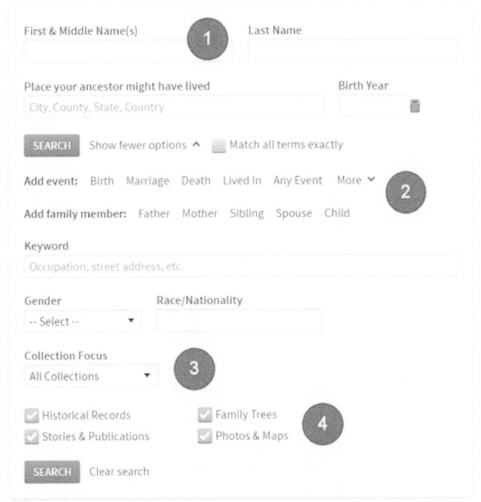

At the top (1) is where you enter the name of the person you are searching for. While we want to find the parents of George W, we don't yet know their names, so we are going to start with George and try to work our way back.

The next two fields – *Place your ancestor might have lived* and *Birth Year* – can safely be ignored. You will be using other fields in the search form.

In the middle (2) are the Event and Family Member widgets. If you click on one of the options, such as Birth or Spouse, the form expands:

First & Middle Name(s)

Last Name

Place your ancestor might have lived

City, County, State, Country

Birth Year

SEARCH   Show fewer options ∧   Match all terms exactly

Add event:   Birth   Marriage   Death   Lived In   Any Event   More ∨

| | Year | Location | |
|---|---|---|---|
| Birth | | City, County, State, Country | × |

Add family member:   Father   Mother   Sibling   Spouse   Child

| | First & Middle Name(s) | Last Name | |
|---|---|---|---|
| Spouse | | | × |

Keyword

Occupation, street address, etc.

You will use these to add details to your search.

Toward the bottom of the form are the *Collection Focus* (3) and *Collection Type* (4) options. You use these to set some initial controls on what is searched. The default is to search everything, but if you know your ancestor only lived in Germany, you can set the Collection Focus to just search German records. Similarly, if you only want to search Historical Records, you can clear the checkboxes on the other Collection Types. For now, keep these at their default settings.

Okay, let's do a search.

In the expanded Global search form, enter the following:

First & Middle Name(s): `George W`

Last Name: `Scott`

Click on the **Birth** event link, and then add

Birth Year: `1890`

Birth Location: `Missouri, USA`

Click on the **Spouse** family member link, and then add
Spouse First & Middle Name(s): Oma
Your search form should look similar to the following:

First & Middle Name(s)

George W

☐ Exact...

Last Name

Scott

☐ Exact...

Place your ancestor might have lived

City, County, State, Country

Birth Year

1890    🖩

☐ Exact +/-...

**SEARCH**    Show fewer options  ^    ☐ Match all terms exactly

**Add event:**   Birth   Marriage   Death   Lived In   Any Event   More ∨

| | Year | Location |
|---|---|---|
| Birth | 1890 | Missouri, USA | ✕ |

☐ Exact +/-...   ☐ Exact to...

**Add family member:**   Father   Mother   Sibling   Spouse   Child

| | First & Middle Name(s) | Last Name |
|---|---|---|
| Spouse | Oma | | ✕ |

☐ Exact

Finally, click the **Search** button. The *Search Results* page appears, showing possible matches for George W Scott.

# THE SEARCH RESULTS PAGE

Let's take a moment to explore the Search Results page:

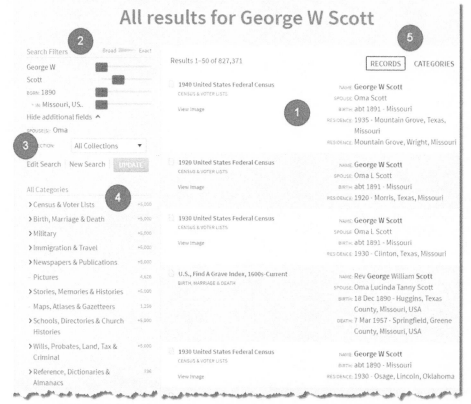

The primary focus is on the *list of records* (1) that match your search criteria. This list is divided into two columns. The left column shows the name of the collection. The collection name is a link. Clicking on it will take you to the *record page*, which is (usually) a partial transcription of the original record. The right side shows summary information from the record. You use this information to see if the record might be about the person you are interested in.

At the top left of the page are the *sliders* (2). These allow you to control how broad or exact your search is. When your search brings back hundreds of thousands of results, you may want to make your search more exact. If you don't get any results, you may need to make it more broad. After you make changes, click the **Update** button.

Below the sliders is the *Edit Search* link (3). Use this to make quick changes to your search criteria without leaving the search results page.

Next, below the sliders and Edit Search link are the *Category Filters* (4). Use these to change the type of records displayed in the search results. If you only want to see the Census & Voter lists, click that link. *Sub-categories*, if available, are displayed, allowing you to further narrow down your search. If you keep drilling down, you will get to a list of collections for a particular category.

Finally, at the top right, are the *Search Results View* links (5). You can switch between the default *Records* view (which is what you are seeing now) and the *Categories* view (which we will review in greater detail later).

## Analyzing the Search Results

There are three census records showing George and Oma Scott, living in Missouri. There is a Find A Grave record showing that George was a reverend. There are some earlier census records that might be George and his parents, but without some additional information, we can't be sure.

Since we know George and Oma were married, we can use the *Category Filters* to look at marriage records for them. That may give us a hint as to who his parents are. In the category filters, click on **Birth, Marriage, & Death**. Then, in the sub-categories, click on **Marriage & Divorce**.

All Categories

Birth, Marriage & Death

  – Birth, Baptism & Christening   +5,000

  – Marriage & Divorce   +5,000

  – Death, Burial, Cemetery & Obituaries   +5,000

In applying the category filters, we have eliminated all search results that aren't in our selected category. The first record is now a marriage record for George W and Oma. The father of George is listed as F H Scott.

Results 1–50 of 53,105

RECORDS    CATEGORIES

Missouri, Marriage Records, 1805-2002
MARRIAGE & DIVORCE

View Image

NAME: George W Scott
SPOUSE: Oma Rattence
FATHER: F H Scott
MARRIAGE: 8 Sep 1910 - Wright, Missouri
CIVIL: Texas, Missouri, USA

We have made a discovery! We now know his father's initials and wife's maiden name. While it would have been nice to have George's father's complete name, we can use his initials as we try to find George with his parents in an earlier census record.

Click on **All Categories** in the Category Filters to go back to the full results, and then click on **Census & Voter Lists** to just look at the census records.

All Categories

> Census & Voter Lists          +5,000

> Birth, Marriage & Death       +5,000

> Military                      +5,000

> Immigration & Travel          +5,000

> Newspapers & Publications      +5,000

If George was born around 1890, then he should be in the 1900 Census with his parents. He may also be in the 1910 Census, if he was still living with them just prior to his marriage. Scanning the search results for 1900 or 1910 Census records for George Scott, born in Missouri, there are a couple of possibilities.

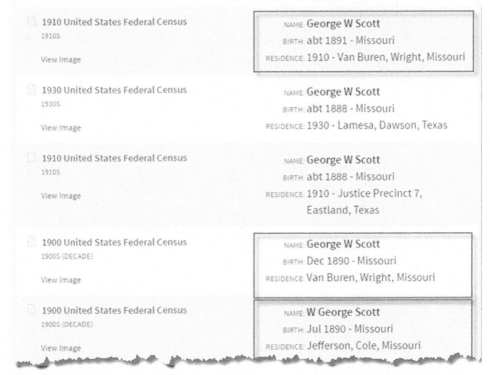

To explore these records further, move your mouse over the collection name. A *record hover* pops up. This preview gives you some insight into the record without having to click through to another page. In doing so, you will see that the 1910 Census shows Foster F Scott as the father of George. The first 1900 Census shows his father as Thomas W Scott. The second 1910 record has Foster F Scott.

Based on the marriage record, we can discount Thomas W Scott as the father. F H in the marriage record doesn't quite match up with Foster F, but transcription errors happen. Based on the current evidence, we make an *assertion* that Foster F Scott and his wife Nancy H Scott are the parents of George W Scott, pending further evidence to the contrary.

## ADDITIONAL NOTES

This was a quick run through of one way to use search and the search results to make a discovery. It was by no means complete or exhaustive. I recommend that you always look at the record transcription in full. If there is an original image for the record, you should always look at that as well. The transcription and image can have more information than is presented in the search results. Additionally, this quick example did not *prove* that these are George's parents, but it does provide some clues for further research.

# THREE GENERAL TYPES OF SEARCH

One more thing before we start going through the tips, although this could be considered a tip. Ancestry has more than one type of search and more than one type of search result list. Knowing about them can help you focus your search and understand the results you see.

There are three broad classifications of search on Ancestry:

- Global
- Category
- Collection-specific

Why should you care? Because using the right search can help you find what you are looking for more effectively.

A *Global* search searches all of the Ancestry collections. (There is a caveat to this claim. See the *Advanced Search Tips* section for more information.) Global search provides a universal starting point for searching. By starting with a global search, you can get a broad overview of the records that are available to explore and then refine your search to focus on specific types of records.

When you are looking for a specific type of information, you might start with a *Category* search. For example, you might want to explore Census records, Birth records, Immigration records, or Military records. Using a Category search helps you reduce the size of the haystack you are searching in. (You will also see that there are sub-categories – such as US Federal Census Collection, or the UK Census Collection – but the concept remains the same.)

If you are looking for a very specific bit of information, and you have enough detail to narrow down when and where you need to look, then you use a *Collection-specific* search. For example, if you know your ancestor was born in California in early 1900s, then searching just the California Birth Index can be more effective than searching all birth records on Ancestry. Again, you are reducing the size of the haystack that you are searching in.

# LOTS & LOTS & LOTS OF SEARCH FORMS

There is only one Global search form. There are a couple hundred Category search forms. There are a couple thousand Collection-specific search forms. Why so many different search forms?

Broadly speaking, every collection is unique. Most of them have a name, but the other details in the collection can be specific only to that collection. For example, you might have a military service number or regiment name in a Civil War collection. Or, you might have the name of a ship in a passenger list collection. When you search an individual collection, these fields are displayed in the search form for that collection, allowing you to focus on the details that are relevant to your search.

Ancestry could create one ginormous search form that contains every possible field from every collection, but that form would be huge and would have a lot of fields that you wouldn't care about for many of your searches. If you are looking for a census record, a field for the military service number is not useful. So, each collection has its own form.

When you search a category, Ancestry takes the most common fields in all the collections in that category and gives you a simplified form that is appropriate to that category. The Census category form is different from the Military category form which is different from the Immigration & Travel category form.

When you search globally, Ancestry takes the most common fields for all of the collections in the entire site and presents them in a single form. (And, yes, there will be fields in that form that do not apply to certain collections – the little grey cells have to do some work as you enter search parameters.)

## SEARCH FORM DESCRIPTIONS

At the bottom of every search Category or Collection-specific search form is a description. Take a moment to read through it the first time you visit a category or collection. You will find out more information on what collections are included in the search and what types of data you might expect to find. This is a frequently overlooked resource. Knowing what you are searching – and if the records you want to search are even there – can make you more effective.

# Two Different Kinds of Search Results

With three different types of search forms, you might expect three different types of search results. Thankfully, there are only two. The more common type is simply referred to as the *search results* page. The less common type is typically referred to as a *collection-specific search results* page (or database-specific search results page).

When you do a Global or Category search, Ancestry shows the records that match your search criteria, displaying the most relevant results first. This is the *search results page*. For a global search, you might see records from census collections, birth collections, probate collections, or any other collection all intermixed. For a category search, you will see records from collections in that category, with the specific collections all intermixed.

Results 1–50 of 60,675

RECORDS     CATEGORIES

1910 United States Federal Census
CENSUS & VOTER LISTS

View Image

NAME: Foster Betsy
BIRTH: abt 1880 - Oklahoma
RESIDENCE: 1910 - Wauhillau, Adair, Oklahoma

1920 United States Federal Census
CENSUS & VOTER LISTS

View Image

NAME: Betsy Ross
BIRTH: abt 1881 - Virginia
RESIDENCE: 1920 - Baltimore Ward 16, Baltimore (Independent City), Maryland

1920 United States Federal Census
CENSUS & VOTER LISTS

View Image

NAME: Betsy Ross
SPOUSE: Albert W Ross
BIRTH: abt 1886 - England
RESIDENCE: 1920 - Cicero, Outagamie, Wisconsin

U.S., School Yearbooks, 1880-2012
SCHOOLS, DIRECTORIES & CHURCH HISTORIES

View Image

NAME: Betsy Ross
BIRTH: abt 1880
RESIDENCE: 1900 - Union Springs, New York, USA

The collection is listed on the left side. Summary information about the record is listed on the right side.

Notice that the summary information is different for each collection. There may be more or less detail for a specific field, or there may be additional fields that show up in some collections and not in others. These search results allow you to review the available information and then view promising records in more detail.

When you do a Collection-specific search, Ancestry presents you with a collection-specific results page. These pages use a columnar display, showcasing key pieces of information in the collection in a format that is easy to scan.

Results 1–49 of 49

| View Record | Name | Gender | Electoral Year | State | District | Subdistrict | View Images |
|---|---|---|---|---|---|---|---|
| View Record | Betsy Ross | Female | 1919 | Victoria | Melbourne Ports | Yarraville | 🖼 |
| View Record | Betsy Ross | Female | 1930 | New South Wales | Robertson | Gulgong | 🖼 |
| View Record | Dorothy Betsy Ross | Female | 1931 | Victoria | Wannon | Portland | 🖼 |
| View Record | Dorothy Betsy Ross | Female | 1931 | Victoria | Wannon | Portland | 🖼 |
| View Record | Betsy Ross | Female | 1932 | New South Wales | Robertson | Gulgong | 🖼 |

Using this page, it is easy to focus in on specific details, which may help you identify the record you are looking for, or which may help you in refining your search.

# Exploring Ancestry for Free

Ancestry is a subscription web site. In order to access the historical records, you must have a subscription. The cost of the subscription to all of Ancestry's content works out to less than the cost of a cup of coffee (or a bottle of soda or water) per day. But, if you just want to kick the tires, you can do a lot of exploration without a subscription. Here are some tips for doing so.

## Some Historical Records are Free

Ancestry provides permanent, free access to over 800 collections. You can search all of the collections at
### *http://search.ancestry.com/search/group/freeindexacom*
If you scroll to the bottom of that page, you can view the full list of free collections. Clicking on one of the collection titles will take you to the Collection-specific search form for that collection.

The collections are listed alpha-numerically. There are several collections that come from other web sites; these are prefixed with "Web" in their titles, so you have to scroll to the bottom to find them. If you don't see a collection covering an area you are looking for, check for it under down in the W's. For example, the *Branch County, Michigan, Death Index* is under *Web* rather than up in the B's. Similarly, there are some prefixed with a country name – US or UK – rather than starting with the state or county. Explore, and you may find some useful records without needing a subscription.

## Special Promotions Provide Free Access

Several times during the year, Ancestry will provide free access to portions of its collections. The specific times and collections may vary by country. For example, Ancestry typically provides free access to Military Collections on Veteran's Day / Remembrance Day. You may see Irish records come up as free around St. Patrick's Day.

If you subscribe to the Ancestry emails, you will typically get a promotional email letting you know what will be offered. These are worth watching for even if you have a subscription. If your subscription is the US Deluxe or UK Deluxe (or another country-specific subscription), these free access weekends may open up some collections you wouldn't otherwise have access to.

## Basic Exploration Without a Subscription

Even without a subscription or a free-access promotion, you can still explore all of Ancestry to see *if* the information you are looking for is available. While you won't be able to see all of the details, you may be able to identify enough information to make progress or to decide to subscribe.

How does this work? When you search on Ancestry, you are searching all of the content, even if you don't have a subscription. The Search Results page will show you results from collections that you don't have permission to view. The results are *veiled*, meaning that some key pieces of information are hidden, and you won't be able to see the full record transcriptions or images. However, if you are using very precise searches, you can make some good deductions without ever seeing all of the details.

## Two Week Free Trial

Finally, Ancestry offers a two-week free trial. This gives you a chance to explore in-depth before starting a regular subscription. As long as you cancel before the end of the two weeks, you won't be charged. If you fail to cancel, your credit card will be charged.

# Part 2: General Search Tips

# GENERAL SEARCH TIPS

Now that you have a handle on basic search strategy, concepts, and terminology, we can dig into the tips that can make you more effective.

This first set of tips apply most broadly. While not every tip will apply to every search form or situation, they apply to many. You should be comfortable using these tips in your day-to-day searches on Ancestry.

## RECOGNIZE THAT ANCESTRY RECORDS ARE (MOSTLY) ABOUT DEAD PEOPLE

At every Family History conference I have worked at, there is always at least one person who comes to the booth and searches for their own name. They get frustrated when they don't find anything.

Don't be that person. The record set for Ancestry is (mostly) for people who have passed away. There are some records for living people – some birth indexes and marriage records are available for those who are still living, and there are people in the 1940 US Federal Census that are still alive today – but the vast majority of records are about those who are deceased.

Ancestry is restricted by the privacy laws and agreements the owners of the records have placed upon them. US Census records are released 72 years after the census was taken; that is a federal statute. UK Census records are released 100 years after the census. States and counties holding marriage or birth records have different local laws or guidelines on when they can be released.

There are exceptions. And if you are looking for your birth parents, it doesn't hurt to try. But in general, you won't find yourself in the Ancestry record set.

# Use the Expanded Global Search Form

When you first use Ancestry, the Global Search form is small, presenting only four fields. The underlying message is "Look how easy this is! We can find really cool stuff about your ancestors if you can just give us a little bit of information!"

While it is true that these four fields are a starting point, your second and third searches should give you more control. To that end, click the "Show more options" link to expand this search form. Ancestry is kind enough to remember this setting for you, so you only have to do it once. Your Global search form should now look like this:

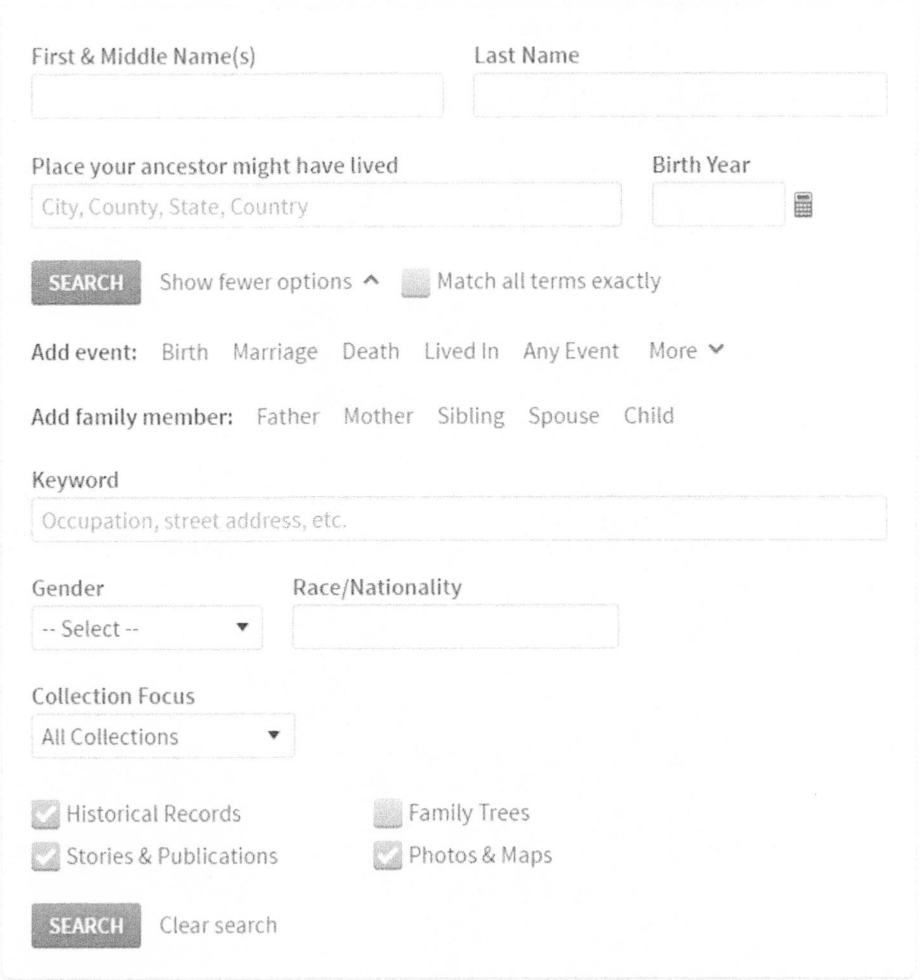

First & Middle Name(s)

Last Name

Place your ancestor might have lived

Birth Year

City, County, State, Country

**SEARCH**    Show fewer options ∧    ☐ Match all terms exactly

**Add event:**    Birth    Marriage    Death    Lived In    Any Event    More ∨

**Add family member:**    Father    Mother    Sibling    Spouse    Child

Keyword

Occupation, street address, etc.

Gender

Race/Nationality

-- Select --    ▼

Collection Focus

All Collections    ▼

☑ Historical Records          ☐ Family Trees
☑ Stories & Publications       ☑ Photos & Maps

**SEARCH**    Clear search

# Reducing the Number of Results – Use the Category Filters

A simple search can return hundreds of thousands (or even millions) of search results. One way to reduce the number of results to something manageable is to use the Category Filters to filter out results that don't apply to what you are currently looking for.

The Category Filters are shown on the left side of the search results page, below the sliders. You can "drill down" into a category to look at very specific types of records – such as only census records from the 1870's, or only Birth &

Christening records. You can also come back up by clicking on any of the higher-level categories.

In the image below, you click on category names below the line to drill down (narrow your search):

> All Categories
>
> > Census & Voter Lists    +5,000
>
> > Birth, Marriage & Death    +5,000
>
> > Military    +5,000
>
> > Immigration & Travel    +5,000
>
> > Newspapers & Publications    +5,000

In the image below, you click on category names above the line to come back up (expand your search):

> All Categories
>
> Birth, Marriage & Death
>
> – Birth, Baptism & Christening    +5,000
>
> – Marriage & Divorce    +5,000
>
> – Death, Burial, Cemetery & Obituaries    +5,000

If you drill down far enough, the Category Filter will display individual collections. Clicking on a collection title will show you only the search results within that collection, and will display the *Collection-specific search results* page.

All Categories

> Birth, Marriage & Death

Birth, Baptism & Christening

- England, Select Births and Christenings, 1538-1975    6923
- Scotland, Select Births and Baptisms, 1564-1950    3857
- The Valley Independent (Monessen, Pennsylvania)    1399

# Looking for Records in the UK? Or Germany? Somewhere Else?

When you are looking for an ancestor who lived in England, sometimes the search will come up with records from the United States (or some other country). To solve this, you can focus your search on just the records in a specific geographic area using the *Collection Focus*.

All Global and Category search forms have a Collection Focus option, as does the Search Results page for Global and Category searches.

Simply select a region, and your search will be limited to those collections from or about that country.

Be aware that this is a sticky setting – it remembers what you have chosen between searches. This can be surprising at times. Imagine that yesterday you were researching in Germany and set the Collection Focus to Germany. When you start your research today, looking for other ancestors in Canada, you may have a hard time finding records until you update the Collection Focus.

Bonus #1: There are ethnic collections on Ancestry. You can restrict your searches to just those collections as well. The three Ethnic collections on Ancestry are African American, Jewish, and Native American.

Bonus#2: If you use the country-specific versions of Ancestry, the Collection Focus is pre-set for you to search just that country. You can change that, but it only remembers the change for the current session (basically, it remembers it for today, but will reset it for tomorrow). To go to a country-specific version of Ancestry, scroll to the bottom of the page and expand the **Visit our other sites** menu:

If you do visit one of these other sites, you will need to log in to that site. Your current Ancestry username and password will work, but you won't have access to any more content than your current subscription allows.

## Go Beyond Names – Adding Events & Places to a Global Search

The simplest – and by far the most common – search on Ancestry is for a name, usually a first name and last name. However, if you know anything else about the person you are searching for, adding that to the search can help the search engine give you more relevant results.

Start with Event. An event is a major happening in a person's life that might get put into an official record. For many of us, that is our birth and marriage. For our ancestors, it includes their deaths. It can include places you have lived at key points in history (such as when a census was taken). Entering or leaving a country, or serving in the military, might also be recorded.

Adding one or more events *that are relevant to the information you are searching for,* can make your search more effective. An event can have two parts – the date when the event happened and the place where the event happened. And they don't have to be precise to be effective.

For example, you may be looking for information on your great-grandmother. You might know she was raised on a farm in Nebraska, but you are not sure where in Nebraska. And you aren't sure when she was born.

Just adding the assumption that she was born in Nebraska can help a great deal. You could start there.

Even if you don't know when she was born, you can probably make a pretty good estimate to help narrow things down. A general rule of thumb is to add 20 years to your age for each generation. Assume you are 30. That would make your parents roughly 50, your grandparents roughly 70, and your great grandparents roughly 90. Subtract that number from the current year, and you have an approximation of a birth year. If your parents are a bit older than that, go back a few extra years. The approximation gives the search engine a place to start from.

To put this in perspective, a global search for Betty White returns over 48 million results. Adding Nebraska to the search reduces this to 37 million. Adding a birth year of 1910 brings us down to 25 million. That's still a lot of results, but using the Category Filters (and some additional tips you will learn), you can bring that number down to a more useful set.

(Of course, the goal isn't to reduce the number of search results to the smallest number. The goal is to help you find the information you are looking for so you can better tell the story of your ancestor. If the first result in the list of 48 million is the one you need, then you don't need to keep digging.)

How do you add an event to the Global search form? Start by clicking on the event name:

First & Middle Name(s)

Last Name

Place your ancestor might have lived

Birth Year

City, County, State, Country

SEARCH   Show fewer options ∧   ☐ Match all terms exactly

Add event:   Birth   Marriage   Death   Lived In   Any Event   More ∨

Add family member:   Father   Mother   Sibling   Spouse   Child

Keyword

Occupation, street address, etc.

Doing so creates a new "row" in the search form. You can add multiple events to your search – just click on another one to add it. The most common ones are shown, and three are hidden under the **More** link (Arrival, Departure, and Military). You can only add one Birth, Marriage, or Death event, but you can add multiple of the other events (like two Lived In events). *However,* keep in mind what you are looking for. Adding your ancestor's death date when looking for a marriage record or a census record probably doesn't help.

# GO BEYOND NAMES & PLACES – ADDING FAMILY MEMBERS TO A GLOBAL SEARCH

Just as adding an event can help focus your search, adding other family members, if known, can also help. Like the Events (discussed above), you can click on the family member (Father, Mother, Sibling, Spouse, or child) to add a row.

Again, be aware of what you are trying to find. If you are looking for your ancestor in a census record with his parents, you probably won't list his children as part of the search. If you are looking for a marriage record, and you know the spouse's name, adding that can help.

As an efficiency tip, you don't need to add last names to most family members. The last name is assumed from the primary person you are searching for. If you are searching for a marriage record or birth record, however, and if you know the maiden name, adding that in can help.

# REDUCING THE NUMBER OF RESULTS – MAKING YOUR SEARCHES MORE PRECISE

By now, you have seen that adding a name or a place to the search form causes an "Exact" option to appear below it. By default, Ancestry casts a broad net to catch as many possible records as reasonably possible. Using the Exact filters, you can tighten that net and bring back more precise results.

The simplest way to tighten the net is on the Search Results page after you have done a search. At the top left of the page are the *sliders*. Simply click and drag one to the right to make the search more exact or to the left to make it more broad. You can adjust several of the sliders before clicking the **Update** button.

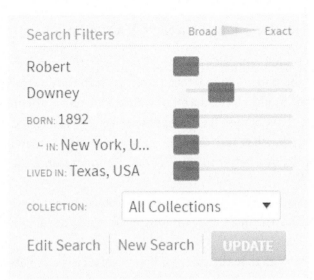

Some tips for using the Exact settings in the sliders:

- Don't mark everything as exact. Odds are, you won't find what you want due to spelling variants.
- Marking places as "Exact to this place" can exclude some records. You may know that William was born in Shropham, Norfolk, England before he moved to the United States, but if you are looking for him *in* the United States, the census won't have that full location and the record won't be found.
- The default setting for last names is actually Exact, expanded to include names that have similar sounds and similar spellings. You can make a last name search broader, if desired, by pulling the slider to the left.
- Dates can be approximate in some records, so be careful when choosing to make it completely exact. Plus or minus 1 or 2 years can often help find records that would otherwise be missed.

Why not use Exact all of the time? Because you may miss out on records that are valid but which have different name or place variants in them. My typical advice is to start somewhat broad, narrow down the category you are looking in, and then start working the sliders.

# Understanding Relevancy Ranked Results: Part 1

When you do a search, Ancestry looks at all of the search terms you provide – names, places, and dates – and matches them up with the documents stored in the index. At the simplest level, if a lot of your search terms are present in a document, then that document is probably one you are interested in. If one document has 10 matches and another document only has 1 match, the first document is probably a better match. For *that particular search*, the first document is more relevant.

Ancestry does some fairly complex calculations to assign a relevancy score to every search result. The most relevant (highest scoring) documents are displayed first.

While you can't change the rules for how relevancy is calculated, you can influence which records are considered relevant.

The simplest way is to use a reasonably complete search. If you look for Bob Smith, you are going to get thousands of records that have the same relevancy score (they all match on the name of Bob Smith). A better search would be for Bob Smith, born around 1920, in Dallas, Texas. If you give the search engine more items to match on, there is a greater chance it will return records that are relevant to you.

If you use the Exact settings, those also affect the relevancy score. An exact match scores higher than a partial match. Adding variants (making the search broader) can catch other name spellings, but will also find lower-scoring records. Of course, if the best match is a variant on the name, then that will float to the top.

However, just because having more terms in your search can help bring back more relevant records, don't go overboard and include every possible term. It is possible to introduce noise into the search. You may net records you don't want or need. It is also possible to include so much information that no records could possibly match the search criteria.

Take a balanced approach. Start with a name, date, and place, if you can. If you are doing a Collection-specific search, then the date may be less important (depending on the collection). If you aren't getting the results you expect, edit the search and add more details, or use the Category filters to further refine your search.

# Location, Location, Location: Part 1

When you start typing a location in the search form, a listing of possible places appears. 99 times out of 100, you want to pick one of the items in the list. And when I say "pick one of the items," I mean exactly that. **When you see the right place, stop typing and click on it.** (Ancestry calls this list the *Place Picker*, and yes, you should pick the place, not type it all in.)

Why? The short answer is that you will get more accurate search results AND you get better filtering options on the location.

The long answer has to do with the way the search engine works. Behind the scenes, places are stored as numbers. Comparing numbers, for a computer, is very efficient – much more efficient that comparing text. All locations in the search engine are stored as numbers. When you pick a location in the place picker, it uses the number for that location. That makes the search faster.

But, even if you don't care how fast the search is, you may care about the accuracy and the filtering options you get. If you just type in a place, the search engine treats it as a bunch of words. It does the best it can to match up your words with the numbers it has in the index, but accuracy can go down.

As for filtering, the Exact options for locations that are picked vs locations that are typed in are different.

With a picked place, the magic number behind the scenes can be compared to other related numbers. When you click **Exact to...**, your options are expanded:

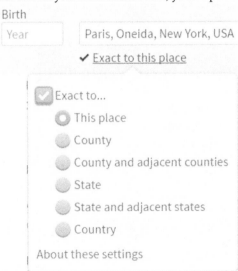

If you just type in a location, your only options are Exact or not Exact.

This shows up well on the sliders on the search results page. With a picked location, multiple options appear in the slider:

If you type in a location, you just get two – broad or exact:

Why should you care about these more specific filters?

- Not all records have complete location information in them. If you enter a full location (city, county, state, country in the case of the United States), the filters help you focus on the right part of the location. For example, US Census records list the birth location as the State or Country. If you are exact on the County or City, you won't find the records.

- City, County, and State boundaries have changed over time. Searching adjacent regions can bring in relevant records that might otherwise be missed.

## STARTING A SEARCH FROM YOUR TREE

If you have a tree on Ancestry, you can easily start a search using the information in your tree. This can be a fast way to start your search process without having to type in everything you know.

You can start a search from a person in your tree three different ways:

First, when you are in the *Tree Viewer*, click on a person to bring up the summary card. Click the **Search** button in the bottom of that card to start a search based on the information you have about that person.

Second, when you viewing the profile page for a person, click the **Search** button in the upper right corner:

Third, just open up a search form and start typing the name of someone in your tree. After the first three characters in the **First Name** field, Ancestry will provide a list of people in your tree that match that name. Ancestry calls this the *Person Picker*, because you pick a person from the list to search on.

First & Middle Name(s)

Har

Harriet Amelia Mosher                          1843–1918

Showing people from:

Sylvia Mosher Family Tree          ▼

(By default, Ancestry looks in the tree you most recently viewed. If you have several trees, you can change the tree by clicking the down arrow in the **Showing people from** list.)

Once you have selected a name, the search form fills with the details from that person:

First & Middle Name(s)

| Harriet Amelia |

☐ Exact...

Last Name

| Mosher McCoy |

☐ Exact...

Place your ancestor might have lived

| City, County, State, Country |

Birth Year

| 1843 |

☐ Exact +/-...

**SEARCH**  Show fewer options ⌃  ☐ Match all terms exactly

Add event:  Birth  Marriage  Death  Lived In  Any Event  More ⌄

| | Year | Location | |
|---|---|---|---|
| Birth | 1843 | Gloversville, Fulton County, New York, USA | ✕ |
| | ☐ Exact +/-...  ☐ Exact to... | | |
| Death | 1918 | Gloversville, Fulton County, New York, USA | ✕ |
| | ☐ Exact +/-...  ☐ Exact to... | | |

Add family member:  Father  Mother  Sibling  Spouse  Child

| | First & Middle Name(s) | Last Name | |
|---|---|---|---|
| Father | Wesson | Mosher | ✕ |
| | ☐ Exact | ☐ Exact | |
| Mother | Mary | | ✕ |
| | ☐ Exact | | |
| Sibling | Sophia Matilda | Mosher | ✕ |
| Sibling | Rachel Cordelia | Mosher | ✕ |

Depending on what you are searching for, you may wish to add or remove details. Or, if everything looks okay, just click the **Search** button.

Note: All of the main search forms on the site support searching from a person in your tree. There are some custom search forms that the Marketing team put together for specific promotions that may not support the Person Picker. (They have been working diligently to replace the older ones that don't use the Person Picker, but it is possible you will find one. If that happens, you will have to (gasp!) type in the details you wish to search for.)

## ADAM OR adam – CASE DOESN'T MATTER IN YOUR SEARCH

While the Hatfields and McCoys may care about how their names are spelled, the search engine doesn't. Hatfield = hatfield = hatFIELD = HaTfEiLd. McCoy = Mccoy = mccoy. My habit is to add an initial capital to most names, but if you want to save yourself a keypress, you don't need to capitalize anything.

Similarly, when you are searching from a person in your tree, the casing of names is ignored. Some people like to put surnames in ALL CAPS in their trees. Others used initial caps. While there are stylistic arguments to be made on both sides of that, from the search engine's perspective, it doesn't matter. Both are resolved to the same underlying search.

So, if your Caps Lock key gets stuck, or if you forget to press the Shift key, it's okay. Your search will still work.

## UPDATE OR EDIT YOUR SEARCH, INSTEAD OF DOING A NEW SEARCH

As I have watched and coached Ancestry customers, one pattern I see frequently is this:

- Doing a search, looking for a census record, typing in multiple details – such as first & last name, birth date, birth place, or spouse's name.
- Reviewing the results, and finding an additional piece of information that would help clarify the search
- Starting a *new search*, typing in all of the information again, plus the new details just discovered

Rather than re-creating your search from scratch each time you want to change it, use the **Edit search** link below the sliders.

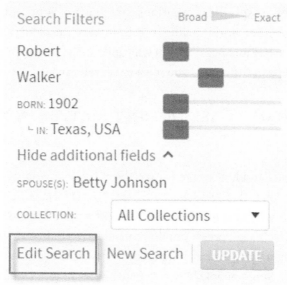

This opens up the search form on top of the current search results page. The search form will have all of your search parameters in it, ready for you to make updates. Click the **Search** button to submit your edited search.

# USE SHORTCUT KEYS ON THE SEARCH RESULTS PAGE TO REDUCE CLICKS

Prefer to use the keyboard? There are some handy shortcut keys that are hidden in plain site on the Search Results page.

Below the Category listing is a link for the **Shortcut Keys**. Click on it to expose the following:

Shortcut Keys ▼

**n** New search

**r** Refine search

**p** Preview current record

**>** Highlight next record

**<** Highlight previous
record

When you are on the Search Result page, pressing one of these keys on your keyboard will perform that action. Need to edit (or refine) your search? Press "r." Want to advance through the available results, highlighting each as you do so? Use the < and > keys. (You don't have to press the shift key – on most US keyboards, these characters are above the comma and period; just press the comma or period key.) Want to see the "record hover" that previews additional information in the record? That's what "p" is for.

Using the < and > keys is a great way to focus your attention on a specific record. It may help you catch details you might otherwise miss in a quick scan.

Also, note that you don't have to open the Shortcut Keys menu to use the shortcut keys. If you forget what one of the keys are, open the menu as a refresher, but you can use the keys with the menu closed.

## INCREASE YOUR PRODUCTIVITY – USING MULTIPLE TABS

This isn't a search tip as much as it is a productivity tip. All modern browsers allow you to have multiple tabs. Almost all modern browsers allow you to open a new tab by holding down the CTRL key when clicking a link (this is usually abbreviated as CTRL + Click).

Once you have narrowed down your search results, there may still be several records to explore. Rather than opening each one, reviewing it, and then going back to the search results, use the CTRL + Click to open each record in a new tab. You can then go to each tab to review the record, explore the image, and make a decision, without ever losing your place in the search results. You can also switch between two or more tabs to compare information. When you are done with a tab, you can close it to keep things neat.

As a bonus tip, you can also click and drag a tab to display it in a new window. This can be helpful when comparing two records, as you can resize windows to put the records side-by-side.

## FINDING SUGGESTIONS IN OTHER PEOPLE'S TREES

You may not be the only person in the world researching your ancestors. By collaborating with others and sharing research, you can reduce the time needed to make discoveries and (potentially) meet and become friends with distant *living* family members.

One way to do this is through the Ancestry Family Trees. There are over 80 million family trees on Ancestry. By searching the Family Trees, you may find suggestions to further your research, stories about your ancestors, and relatives also working on the same family line.

You can directly search other family trees by using the **Public Member Trees** option in the **Search** menu:

The Public Member Trees search form is fairly standard. The Search Results, however, are a bit different:

| Member Tree | Name | Parents |
|---|---|---|
| Results 1–50 of 37,698 | | |
| Robin Pettifer Family Tree<br><br>Public Member Tree<br>2 attached records, 3 sources<br><br>**1** | Roscoe Conkling Hildebrandt<br><br>Birth: 03 Oct 1883 (3 Oct 1883) - Marion, USA<br>Death: 13 August 1939 (13 Aug 1939) - Humboldt, California, USA<br>Marriage: 08 Apr 1905 (8 Apr 1905) - Seattle, King, Washington, USA<br>Spouse: Myrtle Pettifer | F: (Name Unknown)<br>M: (Name Unknown)<br><br>**2** |
| Pettifer Lord Aarstad Hicks/Hartzell Johnson Hartzell Ottini<br><br>Public Member Tree<br>5 attached records, 6 sources photos | Roscoe Conkling Hildebrandt<br><br>Birth: 6 October 1883 (6 Oct 1883) - Marion, USA<br>Death: 13 August 1939 (13 Aug 1939) - Humboldt, California, USA<br>Marriage: 08 Apr 1905 (8 Apr 1905) - Seattle, King, Washington, USA<br>Spouse: Myrtle Dorrit Pettifer | F: Wilhelm Andrew Hildebrandt<br>M: Johanna Louise Eilers<br><br>**3** |
| cameron Family Tree<br><br>Public Member Tree<br>1 source photos | Roscoe Conkling Hildebrandt<br><br>Birth: 06 Oct 1883 (6 Oct 1883) - Marion, USA<br>Death: 13 Aug 1939 - Seattle, King, Washington, USA | F: Wilhelm Andrew Hildebrandt<br>M: Johanna Louise Hannah Eilers |

The left column (1) identifies the name of the tree. Clicking on it will take you to the Profile Page for the person in that tree. Beneath the name are the important bits – the number of attached records, sources, photos, and stories. (If one of these isn't listed, it is because there aren't any attached.) Well documented trees *tend* to be more trustworthy than undocumented trees. Just be sure to look at what the tree owner used for sources and verify that they are actually about the person.

The center column (2) lists a summary for the person in the tree. As the example shows, some are more populated than others, indicating that the person *may* be better researched than in other trees.

The right column (3) shows the parents for the person in the tree. This can be a differentiator in many cases, allowing you to include or exclude these results from further consideration.

From the results, you can determine if you want to visit the profile page for the person. The preview / hover doesn't work on Trees (it displays a not-very-helpful message). Just click through to view the profile page.

A warning, however, about Family Trees. You (and others) are allowed to put whatever information you want into your family tree. You can connect anyone to anyone else. You can attach any record to any person. I hope *you* take the time to analyze connections and to make your family tree as accurate as possible, but not everyone does. *Just because there is a family tree with your ancestor in it, don't assume that the tree, or even that the information for that person, is 100% correct.* You must do your own analysis. I like to say that everyone is entitled to their own family mythology. You may find a tree that takes you back to Adam or the King of Moldovia, but you should check the documentation and sources for those trees. Use trees as a pointer to further your own research, but don't blindly accept the information in someone else's tree as true.

Finally, if you find yourself coming back to a "trusted" tree, consider contacting the owner of the tree. At the top of every profile page is a link to the tree owner:

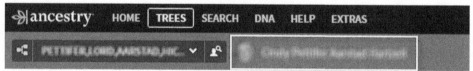

Click on the name to go to the member directory page for that person. On the top right of that page is a large orange button:

Click that to send a personal message through the *Ancestry Messaging System.* This allows you to send and receive messages without sharing your email address. (Of course, once you get to know a person, you may choose to communicate in other ways.)

# Part 3: Intermediate Search Tips

# Intermediate Search Tips

You should now be comfortable with the basics of search on Ancestry. It is time to go a bit deeper to take greater control of your searches. This section will help you become more efficient and help you make the most of your Ancestry subscription.

## Effective Use of the Keyword Field

Every Ancestry search form has a Keyword field in it. Most people don't use it. Most of the time, that is a good thing. However, it can be useful.

The Keyword field is a catch-all field. If you search for "Peaches" as a Keyword, you will find records where Peaches is a name, a place, a street address, or an item for sale in the Sears Catalog. It searches every indexed field in your search scope. If you are doing a Global search, it searches every field in every collection. It can help you find some rare gems; it can also find records you really didn't want.

The Keyword field also lets you search fields that aren't displayed on the search form. For example, in the 1930 Census, the Street Address is indexed in the search engine, but there aren't enough records with a street address to display a Street Address field in the search form. But if you search for `Main Street` in the Keyword field (and set it to Exact), you can find those addresses.

When should you use the keyword field? It will depend on the content you are searching in. Street names are a good option, if you know the collection has street names. Parish names are good in some of the UK collections. If you are searching newspapers or family histories, then using the Keyword field with an Exact setting can help narrow down the results; similarly, searching for business names, addresses, locations, or events (such as elections, disasters, or parades) can help you find related information.

If doing a regular search isn't finding what you are looking for, moving some of the details to the Keyword field on the search form may give you a breakthrough.

# The Lived In Event & the Any Event

The Global search form and some of the Category search forms have two Event options that can be helpful, but only if you use them carefully.

The Lived In event is sort of like it sounds – my ancestor lived in or *resided* in this place. A Census lists who lived in a particular place at a particular time. A birth implies a residence, since the child lived there when they were born. It is broader than selecting one of the other specific events, but not as broad as the Any Event.

The Any Event is trickier. Ancestry classifies several event types, and many records have multiple events in them. The Any Event will match – are you ready for this? – any of them.

Consider a 1911 England Census record for Robert Walker. The Census identifies where Robert was living in 1911. That is a Residence Event. It identifies when and where he was born. That is a Birth Event.

Or look at the Death collections. Most death records have a Death Event. Many also list a Birth Event. Some could list a Marriage Event. If there is a last known address, there may be a Residence Event.

When you search in the Any Event field, you are asking for any record that has a place and/or a date in it. If you don't otherwise narrow your search down, you will get a lot of results, and some of them will look strange.

In general, I recommend using a specific event. If aren't sure which event may have taken place, then try the Lived In event. If that doesn't open things up enough, then try the Any Event.

# Understanding Relevancy Ranked Results: Part 2

You already know that results are listed in order, with the most relevant records listed first. And you have probably done searches where the results don't seem to have any relation to the person you were looking for. How could the search engine return something that – to a human – is so obviously wrong?

As a specific example, search in the 1930 US Federal Census for Ann Smith. (Yes, I recognize this is a bad search, but it showcases the issue.) The first three results are shown below:

| | | | | | | | |
|---|---|---|---|---|---|---|---|
| View Record | Ann Bloomfield | Martha | Shelby, Richland, Ohio | abt 1863 | New York | Head | |
| View Record | Lydia N Corbett ✎ | Paul F | Kamiah, Idaho, Idaho | abt 1878 | Idaho | Wife | |
| View Record | Elizabeth Crina ✎ | William J | Hoopeston, Vermilion, Illinois | abt 1864 | Indiana | Wife | |
| View | Elizabeth Ann | George, | Fargo, Cass, North | abt | North | | |

You searched for Ann Smith, but none of these results are for Ann Smith! How could this happen? Must be something wrong with the search engine, right?

Actually, it is a problem with the search results display. Digging deeper, you will actually see that that is a match. If you click through to view the results, you will see that there are alternate names provided for these records:

Name: Ann Bloomfield
[Ann Smith]

Name: Lydia N Corbett
*[Lydia Ann Smith]*

Name: Elizabeth Crina
*[Elizabeth Crain]*
*[Elizabeth Ann Smith]*
[Elizabeth Criner]

In the first one, an alternate keyed name – *Ann Smith* – was provided by the system. These can occur when:

- Ancestry makes an update to a collection to correct mis-transcribed records
- Ancestry partners with another company on the index and both indexes are used to increase findability

The second one has a user-contributed alternate name. *Lydia Ann Smith* is provided as a Maiden Name variant.

The last one has two user-contributed alternates as well as a system provided alternate.

In all cases, *Ann Smith* is a valid match. The record contains a reference to Ann Smith as an alternate value, but those names don't show up in the search results.

Just because the results look weird, don't assume the engine got it wrong. There could be some additional data behind the scenes that is promoting the result.

## SEEING WHICH COLLECTIONS HAVE RESULTS – USING THE CATEGORIES VIEW

By default, Ancestry displays search results with the most relevant results listed first. The **Records** view always displays the most relevant records first.

The **Categories** view, however, does not. In the Categories view, collections are grouped and listed by result count (the collections with the most results are listed first) or alphabetically (the collections are listed by name).

Use the Categories view when you want to quickly see which collections have search results and to look in specific collections. For example, if you have found census records for your ancestor in the 1900, 1920, and 1930 Census collections, you may want to only look in the 1910 and 1940 collections. The Categories view provides an easy way to see if there are results in those collections and gives you a one-click entry point into those collections. (Clicking into a collection takes you to the Collection-specific results view.)

To get to the Categories view, simply click the Categories link at the top of the Search Results page:

If you have done a Global search, then the Categories and top collections in each category are listed. At the bottom of each category is a link to view all of the collections containing search results in that category:

| 103,088,369 results | RECORDS | CATEGORIES |

| Census & Voter Lists | 17,866,868 |
| 1940 United States Federal Census | 1,390,102 |
| 1930 United States Federal Census | 1,304,342 |
| Australia, Electoral Rolls, 1903-1980 | 1,200,397 |
| 1920 United States Federal Census | 1,149,868 |
| 1910 United States Federal Census | 1,037,496 |

See all 17,866,868 results...

| Birth, Marriage & Death | 30,115,557 |
| England, Select Births and Christenings, 1538-1975 | 1,900,545 |
| England & Wales, Civil Registration Birth Index, 1916-2005 | 1,806,425 |
| U.S., Find A Grave Index, 1600s-Current | 1,463,799 |
| U.S., Social Security Applications and Claims Index, 1936-2007 | 1,386,538 |
| England & Wales, Civil Registration Birth Index, 1837-1915 | 941,996 |

See all 30,115,557 results...

| Military | 3,045,356 |
| U.S. Marine Corps Muster Rolls, 1798-1958 | 427,251 |

Starting a search from a Category, or clicking through into a category list, gives you a full list of the collections which contain results. By default, this list is sorted by the number of results. You can, however, sort them by name, which puts the collections into alpha-numeric order:

| 17,866,868 results | RECORDS | CATEGORIES |

Sort by name | results count

| 1770-1790 Census of the Cumberland Settlements | 26 |
| 1790 United States Federal Census | 6,230 |
| 1790-1850 Town census of Clifton Park, Half Moon, Waterford, Niskayuna | 53 |
| 1800 census, Clinton County, New York | 1 |
| 1800 census, Delaware | 68 |
| 1800 United States Federal Census | 8,194 |
| 1810 census, Augusta County, Virginia | 4 |

What you should know about the Categories view:

- The collections in the Categories view are *not* listed in relevancy ranked order. They are listed by the number of records which could match your search. When you click through into a collection, the records from that collection are listed in relevancy ranked order.
- Clicking on a collection in the Categories view will take you to the Collection-specific search results page for that single collection.
- Using CTRL+Click to open the collection in a new tab is a handy way to keep your place in the Categories view.
- The collections can be sorted by name or by results count *only when you are looking at a single category*.
- You can (and should) use the Category filters (on the left of the page) to further refine or expand the list of collections you are looking at.

## USE WILDCARDS FOR MANGLED OR OFTEN MISSPELLED NAMES

Wildcards are one of the least used search features on Ancestry, probably because there are no direct instructions for how to use them in the search form. (There is a link at the bottom of the **Exact...** options on the first and last name fields that opens a help window. At the bottom of that window is information on using wildcards, but very few people look there, and even fewer of them expect to see anything about wildcards.)

A wildcard is used to replace letters in your searches. If you are not sure if an ancestor went by Bill or Will, you could do two separate searches, or you could use a wildcard to replace the first character. Or, if the census takers might have taken liberties with your ancestor's last name – Pennington, Peningtoon, Pennytown – you can use a wildcard to replace multiple characters.

Key things to know about wildcards:

- The question mark (?) replaces a single character.
- The asterisk (*) replaces 0 or more characters.
- You can use more than one wildcard in the same word.
- You can use both types of wildcards in the same word.
- The case of the letters do not matter (they can be upper or lowercase)

In any case, **you must have at least three non-wildcard characters in the word** and **the first character cannot be a wildcard**, or the search engine will reject the query and tell you that you have too many wildcards in your query.

You can use wildcards in the following fields in Global search or a Category search:

- Any name field (such as First Name, Last Name, or Father's First Name)
- The Keyword field
- The Race / Nationality field

When you get into collection-specific search forms (such as the search form for the 1930 US Federal Census), there are other fields you can use wildcards in. For example, **Relation to Head of House** would allow you to search for `step*` – that would find any stepbrothers, stepsisters, stepsons, etc.

You cannot use wildcards with locations or dates.

Examples:

`?ill` – finds records containing Bill or Will. It will also find records contain Dill, Mill, and Pill. Any name that starts with a letter followed by `ill` are valid matches. It will NOT find `ill` on its own – the `?` wildcard assumes that is replacing a single letter.

`C??per` – finds records containing Cooper, Couper, and Cruper. The two wildcards are replaced with any other two characters.

`Will*` – finds records containing Will, Willy, William, Willford, or any other word that starts with `Will`. Note that the `*` matches 0 or more characters; `Will` is a valid match in this.

`P*t*n` – finds Peterson, Petersen, Pantaloon, and similar names. If it starts with a P, contains a T, and ends with an N, it is a valid match.

# WHEN TO MAKE AN EXACT SEARCH A FUZZY SEARCH

Exact generally means "completely precise." Ancestry extends that definition to "completely precise, unless you want us to be less precise and find other variants for you."

If you mark a search term as Exact, it will look for that precise term in the indexed records. But this is not always what you want. Sometimes, you need the search to be fuzzy and mostly match your terms. Let's look at an example.

If you search for Robert Peterson and make the first name and last name fields exact, then Ancestry:

- Looks for records that match Robert in the First Name field and Peterson in the Last Name field

That is what you would expect Exact to do – only find records that have both Robert and Peterson as a name.

But what if Robert sometimes went as Rob or Bob? What if the census enumerator spelled his last name as Petersen? Would you want to find those records as well? You want to find records about Robert Peterson, regardless of how his name was spelled. By making your Exact searches fuzzy, you can.

Extending this example, you can have Ancestry do the following:

- Looks for records for Robert Peterson
- Looks for records that have variants of Robert and Peterson
- Looks for records for Peterson
- Looks for records for variants of Peterson

There are three ways to fuzzify your search (no, I did not make up that word, but I wish I had):

1. Use the Exact options on the Search Forms to fuzzify Names, Dates, and Places
2. Use the Sliders on the Search Results pages to fuzzify Names, Date, and Places
3. Use Exact with Wildcards fuzzify Names

## USE THE EXACT OPTIONS FOR NAMES, DATES, AND PLACES

When you select Exact for a Name, Date, or Place in a search form, a popup menu gives you some additional options. When you select from these options, you are fuzzifying the search.

Similarly, you fuzzify the search from the search results page, by using the sliders to adjust your search precision.

You can specify name variants. Searches must return records that contain one of the variants. Use this to catch alternate spellings, diminutives, similar sounding names, or initials.

You can specify date ranges. Use this to account for approximations in the record (census records may be off by a year or two). You should also keep in mind that some people didn't age as fast as others – while the census came around every 10 years, there are men and women who only aged 4 or 6 years in that period (age 22 in 1900, 28 in 1910, 34 in 1920...you get the idea). Self-reporting and creative uncertainty over birthdates means dates can be off. Start with a narrow range, but be ready to expand it.

You can specify place variants. When you type in a place in the search form, the form will provide a list of places. PICK ONE OF THE SUGGESTIONS. Doing so enables the Exact options for the place, and you can search in a specific city, in the county, in the surrounding counties, in the state, in the surrounding states, or in the country. Select the one that is appropriate to the record set you are searching.

## USE EXACT WITH WILDCARDS ON NAMES

While it may seem odd, you can also use wildcards with Exact when you are searching for names. This allows you to find records with exact matches to one of the allowed wildcarded terms. For example, a search for Jon* in the first name field requires that the record match Jon, Jonny, or Jonas. This gives you some control over what is searched for, rather than relying exclusively on the variants generated by the search engine.

Conversely, when you use wildcards, those other variants on the name are not applied by the search engine. For example, a regular search for Jon could find variants on the name, such as John or Jonathan. Adding a wildcard would not expand the search to look for those variants. A search for Jon* would not find John.

# Other Tips for Using Exact

Names, Dates, and Places give you several different Exact options. Other fields only give you an Exact checkbox. On the Global Search form, these fields include Keyword, relative's names (such as Father's name, Mother's name, or Spouse's name), and Race/Nationality. On the Category and Collection-specific search forms, any field that is not the primary name, a date, or a location should offer an Exact checkbox.

If you check the box, then that term MUST appear in that field in the record exactly as you typed it.

Unless, of course, you use a wildcard. Then one of the allowed variants of that term must appear in that field in the record.

Or, unless you specified two or more words in the field. In that case, then all words must appear somewhere in the field (order doesn't matter).

Some uses for using Exact in these other fields:

- Specifying a father, mother, spouse, sibling, or child in a census search
- Finding others who served in the same Military Unit. For example, if you know your great grand uncle Robert served in the Oxfordshire Light Infantry, you can search the WWI Service records for others who may have served with him by doing an exact search on the regiment name
- Finding variants of Ship Names on passenger lists
- Finding a street name in the 1940 US Federal Census
- Finding a relationship in many of the census records (`step*` or `*inlaw` are good variants)

Many of these require that you become familiar with the collections you are searching, and that is a good thing.

# Specifying Gender in your search

Many of the search forms allow you to specify a gender (male or female). This appears fairly straightforward. You search for Pat Smith, Female. You should get records where Pat Smith is a female and not a male. For collections that actually specify the gender, or for which the gender can be inferred, such as the census or many marriage records, this works perfectly. For some collections, however, you may see men showing up in the list. Why?

Because the underling search is actually an exact search for all records where Pat Smith is not male or has no gender assigned. If you flipped the search to male, then it would be for records where Pat Smith is not female or has no gender assigned.

This allows Ancestry to return more records which *may* potentially match. For example, a passenger list may not specify a gender. An exact search for the specified gender would eliminate records that didn't specify a gender, which could hide records relevant to your search.

Why a "not male" or "not female" search? Jump ahead to the *Advanced Search Tips* section for a discussion on Exact = Required if you want the nitty-gritty details.

## Specifying Race/Nationality in your search

Many of the search forms allow you to specify the Race or Nationality. For global and category searches, you should generally avoid this. For collection-specific searches, you can use it, but you should be aware of the way race is represented in the collection.

For example, the 1930 US Federal Census has instructions for the enumerators on how different races should be noted. The 1940 Census is a bit different. And the 1911 England Census doesn't specify gender. White could mean Caucasian, but Caucasian Hawaiian isn't the same. Black, Negro, and Mulato were common references in some collections, and there is one collection that actually uses 10 different "shades" to represent race. Before using Race/Nationality in your search, and especially before marking it as Exact, you should review the information about the collection and examine some of the images, which may provide a reference key. Even then, you must recognize that enumerators didn't always follow instructions. There are Blacks and Negros in the 1940 Census, even though the instructions were clear to use "Negro." Similarly, some people of Asian descent might be correctly recorded as Chinese or Korean or Japanese. They might also be listed as "yellow." While these terms are not correct in modern society, if you use this field, you must be aware of the historical context of the records you are looking for.

If you are searching from the Global or Category search form, you should also be aware that some collection-specific fields are mapped to the race/nationality field. For example, in the US Indian Census Rolls, there is a field for Tribe. This is mapped to race/nationality. A search for `blue` will find results for members of the Blue Lake tribe, which may or may not be what you expected.

As a side note, and further proof that enumerators didn't follow instructions in all cases, or where transcribers made mistakes, you can find the following examples of race/nationality:

- Green
- Blue (and not a member of the Blue Lake tribe)
- Spanish
- Orange
- Wet
- Damp
- Dead (in a marriage record!)

Use this feature with care. It can help, but overuse may exclude valid records simply because the enumerator was thinking differently than you do.

# Searching from Your Tree – Gaining Control

Searching from your tree is a great way to "start with what you know." Everything about the person you started your search from is added to the search, which can save some typing. But there are also some pitfalls and tips you should be aware of to make the process more effective.

## Smart Filtering

Imagine this: You are searching the Census collection for Della Scott, born in 1895 in Missouri, USA. After sorting through the numerous records in the 1900 Census, you find the correct one and attach it to her tree. Later, you search for more records about her, and the first 10 results are all from the 1900 Census. You don't need any more records from the 1900 Census for her, but you have to wade through them to get to the records you do need.

Thankfully, Ancestry implemented Smart Filtering. If you have attached a record to a person in your tree, and if you search from that person, then similar records from the same collection are filtered out of the search results. Generally, your ancestor only appears once in each census, so filtering out all results from censuses you have attached will allow other records to rise to the top. (And, yes, there are exceptions – I have an ancestor that moved between enumeration districts and got counted twice.)

The records already attached to the person in your tree are listed at the top of the search results:

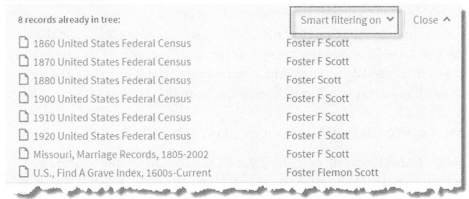

8 records already in tree:          Smart filtering on ⌄    Close ⌃

📄 1860 United States Federal Census          Foster F Scott

📄 1870 United States Federal Census          Foster F Scott

📄 1880 United States Federal Census          Foster Scott

📄 1900 United States Federal Census          Foster F Scott

📄 1910 United States Federal Census          Foster F Scott

📄 1920 United States Federal Census          Foster F Scott

📄 Missouri, Marriage Records, 1805-2002      Foster F Scott

📄 U.S., Find A Grave Index, 1600s-Current    Foster Flemon Scott

If you want to re-check these specific collections, you can turn Smart Filtering off – just click **Smart filtering on** and then choose the option to turn it off. Turning off is a temporary setting.

What types of records are used in Smart Filtering? The general classification is collections where the person is only expected to be found once. Census collections, military drafts, birth collections, and death collections are included. Marriage collections are not. While you may know that your ancestor was only married once, it is *possible* for him to have been married multiple times, so those collections are not filtered.

As a point of clarification, if you find a birth record in one collection, then only birth records from that collection are filtered out. If there is another collection that also has a birth record for your ancestor, it will show up (until you find it and attach it to your tree).

## LOCATION, LOCATION, LOCATION: PART 2 – SEARCHING FROM YOUR TREE

When you search from your tree, locations are filled in as a bunch of words. As you may recall from our earlier discussion, this limits your filtering options in the **Exact to...** settings and in the sliders on the Search Results page.

Whenever you do a search from a person in your tree (or whenever you select a person in your tree while in a search form), if the location is important to you, you *must* edit the search to "fix" the locations.

To do this, click **Edit Search** below the sliders (or press "r" on your keyboard), click in the location field, and click on one of the locations that appear. Even it is exactly the same as what is in the form, click on it. This will enable the **Exact to...** options in the search form for that location. Clicking **Search** to apply the changes also enables the location slider in the search results.

As a reminder, the **Exact to...** options allow you to control how exact the search is on the location – you can specify the full city, county, state, and country, but search for records in the county, in surrounding counties, in the state, or in surrounding states (as well as those that specify the city).

## REMOVE INFORMATION THAT DOESN'T APPLY TO YOUR SEARCH

Filling a search form with everything you know is not always the best strategy, but that is what happens when you search from a person in your tree. Using the information from your tree as a starting point can be efficient, but it can also introduce extra noise into the search and bring back extraneous results.

For example, if you are looking for the 1880 US Federal Census record for someone born in 1865, including that person's spouse and children in the search probably doesn't help. Including the parents does. This individual was most likely not married at 15 years old and was probably living with his or her parents.

Alternately, if you are looking for the 1920 US Federal Census record for this same individual, the spouse and children may be useful discriminators in your search, while the parents are not.

This goes back to the core strategy of knowing what you want to find. If you are looking for a marriage record, there probably aren't children listed. If you are looking for a death certificate, parents or spouse may be included. Military records are typically only about the service member. Some travel documents may have family relationships; others will not. Think about what you are looking for and what information makes sense to include.

How do you remove extra information from a search? Quite simply. In the Search Results page, click **Edit Search** below the sliders (or press "r" on your keyboard). This brings up the search form with all of your search parameters in it.

Next to each person or location is an "X." Clicking that will clear the value:

Note: This doesn't remove the person or place from your tree. It just removes them from the current search.

What are the ramifications of including everyone and every place in your search? It depends. The biggest risk is finding records that are less about the person you are looking for. Consider a search for Flemmon Scott, born in 1819 in Missouri. Flemmon and his wife Phebe were fecund, with children Malinda, Polly, Gabriel, Joseph, Sarildah, Sarah, Greenup, Foster, and George. Including all of the children in the search when looking for birth information for Flemmon will bring back results, but the results will be for others who match the children's names. (There are no direct birth records for Missouri for this time period.)

If I accidently find a birth record for one of Flemmon's children while looking for his birth information, is that bad? Not necessarily – serendipitous discovery can be exciting. But you should understand what is happening. Generally, you will want to include the appropriate search criteria for what you are looking for.

## Explore by Location

One of the least used but most useful search features on Ancestry is Explore by Location. Since it is buried below the Global search form, most people never see it.

This feature shows you all of the collections available on Ancestry for a particular geographic region. Want to know what collections have records covering Albany, New York? Or perhaps in Oaxaca, Mexico? What about collections for Belgium? Explore by Location provides this. You can quickly find the collections that apply to your particular search project. You may also discover that Ancestry doesn't have the particular collection you need. Knowing that can help reduce time spent searching for something that can't yet be found on the site.

From Explore by Location, you can search a single interesting collection using the Collection-specific search form. It is a great tool for finding out what collections are available, which can save you time and frustration.

There are two different versions of this feature – one for the US (the Ancestry.com site) and one for all of the other country sites (such as Ancecstry.co.uk).

# EXPLORE BY LOCATION – US

To get to the Explore by Location feature, click on **Search** in the header, and then scroll down to the static map:

Explore by Location

USA    UK & IRELAND    EUROPE    CANADA    AUSTRALIA & NZ

United States

Recent additions include:

- 1940 United States Federal Census - **New**
- 1930 United States Federal Census - **Updated**
- U.S. City Directories (Beta)

| | | | | | |
|---|---|---|---|---|---|
| Alabama | Florida | Louisiana | Nebraska | Oklahoma | Vermont |
| Alaska | Georgia | Maine | Nevada | Oregon | Virginia |
| Arizona | Hawaii | Maryland | New Hampshire | Pennsylvania | Washington |
| Arkansas | Idaho | Massachusetts | New Jersey | Rhode Island | West Virginia |
| California | Illinois | Michigan | New Mexico | South Carolina | Wisconsin |
| Colorado | Indiana | Minnesota | New York | South Dakota | Wyoming |
| Connecticut | Iowa | Mississippi | North Carolina | Tennessee | USA |
| Delaware | Kansas | Missouri | North Dakota | Texas | |
| District of Columbia | Kentucky | Montana | Ohio | Utah | |

This page is the entry point into Explore by Location. You can change the map displayed to a different region by clicking one of the regions above the map:

Click on any of the states or regions on the map (or listed below the map) to explore the collections Ancestry has available for that location *and to expand or focus on other regions not shown on the map.*

## EXPLORING THE COLLECTIONS IN A SPECIFIC REGION

After you click an item in the map, the page displays a list of the top collections available on Ancestry for the selected region. The collections are clustered by available type – Census, BMD, Military, Directories, Wills, etc. Each collection name is listed, and the number of records available in that collection is also shown.

United Kingdom Census & Voter Lists
Slave Registers of former British Colonial Dependencies, 1813-1834 `FREE`   2,980,774
1851 United Kingdom Census Sample   994,793
**View other** Census & Voter Lists collections related to United Kingdom. (68)

United Kingdom Birth, Marriage & Death
UK and Ireland, Find A Grave Index, 1300s-Current `FREE`   4,704,322
England & Wales, Non-Conformist and Non-Parochial Registers, 1567-1970   2,530,704
Web: UK, Burial and Cremation Index, 1838-2014 `FREE`   1,610,623
JewishGen Online Worldwide Burial Registry (JOWBR) `FREE`   1,195,945
Web: Global, Gravestone Photograph Index, 1265-2014 `FREE`   876,327
**View all** United Kingdom Birth, Marriage & Death (18)

In the example above, two categories are shown – **Census & Voter Lists** and **Birth, Marriage & Death** records. The top collections by record count for that category are listed. At the bottom of each category is a link to **View other collections**. Clicking that will bring up a list of all the collections in that category for the selected geographic region.

Clicking on an any collection takes you to the Collection-specific search form for that collection.

In the upper right of the page, there is also a button to search only collections applicable to the current geographic region:

Clicking this **Search** button brings up the Global search form, with the Location value preset to get you started.

CHANGING THE GEOGRAPHIC REGION YOU ARE EXPLORING

The right side of the page has tools that you use to change the region you are looking at.

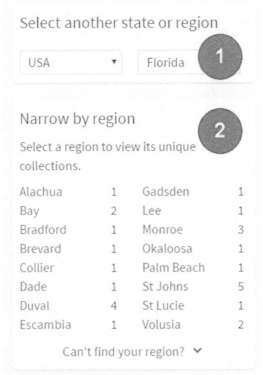

Use the first (1) tool to change to another region – including those that aren't listed on the introductory maps.

Use the **Narrow by region** (2) to go deeper into the collection set. If you are looking in US States, you can find collections that have records for a specific county. (Please note that not all countries have a sub-region represented in the Ancestry collection set; if this is the case for the country you have selected, the **Narrow by region** section will not be shown.)

# EXPLORE BY LOCATION – ANYWHERE BUT THE US

This is one of the areas where the Ancestry.com site is behind the other sites. I find this map much easier to use. I will often go to one of the country sites just to use this version of Explore by Location.

To get to the Explore by Location feature, click on **Search** in the header, and then scroll down to the dynamic map:

| | | | | |
|---|---|---|---|---|
| Armenia | Denmark | Ireland | Netherlands | Spain |
| Austria | England | Isle of Man | Northern Ire... | Sweden |
| Belarus | Estonia | Italy | Norway | Switzerland |
| Belgium | Finland | Latvia | Poland | Turkey |
| Bosnia | France | Liechtenstein | Portugal | Ukraine |
| Channel Isla... | Germany | Lithuania | Romania | Wales |
| Croatia | Gibraltar | Luxembourg | Scotland | Yugoslavia |
| Cyprus | Hungary | Malta | Slovakia | |
| Czech Repu... | Iceland | Moldova | Slovenia | |

The map reflects your current location, but you can jump to other locations using the links immediately below the map. In the example above, Europe is highlighted; click on Oceania to change the focus of the map to Australia and New Zealand.

Each library icon  represents a collection set for that area. Hovering your mouse over the icon will give you name of the region and the number of collections available.

You can zoom in on the map to see if there are sub-sets.

When you click on a library icon (or click on one of the links below the map), the full Explore by Location page opens:

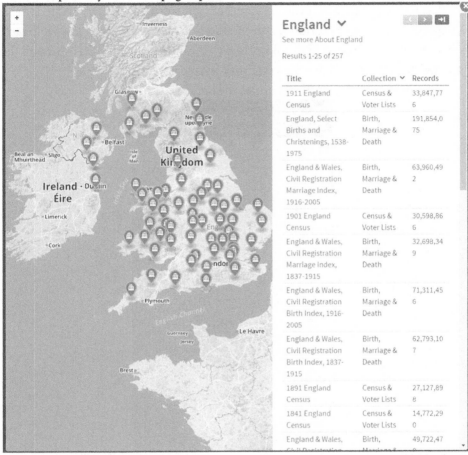

The map remains interactive – keep zooming and panning around to look at the region of interest. At any time, click on one of library icons. The collections for that area are then displayed in the panel on the right. Click a collection to search just that collection.

At the top of the panel, you can click the current top-level region (in the example above, that is England) to use a menu to change the region. Similarly, you can click on **Collection** at the top of the list to filter the collections to a particular type (such as Census, BMD, or Military).

# NARROWING YOUR SEARCH – USING THE CARD CATALOG

The Ancestry Card Catalog provides another view into the Ancestry collections. Where the Explore by Location feature focuses on finding collections specific to a geographic region, the Card Catalog gives you multiple ways to filter through the 32,000+ collections available for searching on Ancestry.

The Card Catalog is available under the Search menu:

Why use the Card Catalog? Remember the basic search strategy – start with what you know, identify what you want to know, and then search the most likely places for that information. *Using the Card Catalog, you can focus your search on the areas that are most likely to have what you need.* When you have found a collection of interest, you can limit your search to just that collection.

Every collection name is a link to the Collection-specific search form for that collection. Once you have found a collection, use CTRL+Click to open the search form in a new tab. You can open several potential collections this way and then search them individually.

How do you find the collection you need? There are three primary methods:

1. Sort the collection list
2. Search the collection list
3. Filter the collection list

These methods can be combined. For example, you could filter the collection list and then change how the collection list is sorted in the filtered set.

## SORTING THE COLLECTIONS

By default, Ancestry presents the list of collections in Popularity order. The most-frequently used collections are listed first. This can give you a feel for what others are finding success in, but there are other ways to sort that are also helpful.

To change how the collections are sorted, use the **Sort By** option at the top right of the Card Catalog:

If you have filtered the collections, then listing by **Database Title** can be a good choice. The collections are sorted alpha-numerically, which may help with scanning the available collections. For example, if you have filtered on US Censuses from the 1800s and sort by title, then the oldest collections are listed first (since most start with a date), and you get a timeline view of the collections.

**Date Updated** will show you collections that have been recently updated on Ancestry. Updated collections may contain new information or may simply have portions of the index corrected. The most recently updated collections are listed first. Use this to see what is new and to see if you may need to take another look at collections you have explored in the past. (This also lists new collections.)

**Date Added** shows the most recently added collections on Ancestry. The newest collections will have a **New** tag next to them; typically, the **New** tag on these collections lasts for three months. If you have completed much of your research, you can check in periodically to see what is new and decide if you need to renew your subscription to explore those new collections.

**Record Count** is mostly a gee-whiz feature. Sorting the collections by the total number of indexed records is interesting, but not terribly useful in most cases. If you have filtered the collection set down and want to search the largest collection, then a record count sort can help. However, I find that if I have done a good job of filtering, I can scan the list just as efficiently without needing to sort by record count.

## SEARCHING THE COLLECTIONS

The Card Catalog is searchable. That doesn't mean you can search the collections from the Card Catalog. It does mean that you can search the Card Catalog for collections that may be useful to you.

There are two search fields in the Card Catalog: **Title** and **Keyword**.

Title

Keyword(s)

SEARCH or Clear All

Do NOT use both fields at the same time. Use one or the other, and then filter/sort as needed. (If you do use both, the world won't end, but you probably won't get the results you expect.)

These search fields are relatively simple. They look for exact matches. If you search for Marriage in the **Title** field, it will find collections that contain Marriage in the title. It will not find Marriages. There are 300+ Marriage collections and 400+ Marriages collections.

You can use the * and ? wildcards to get around this simplicity. A search for Marriage* will return all 850 collections.

The **Keyword** field allows you to search through the collection description. It is not as precise, but it can be easier to use. For example, you may not remember the title of a specific collection, but you know what it is about. A search for

`Regiment` in the **Keyword** field will bring back a set of military collections that refer to regiments, but which may not use Regiment in the title.

Like the Title field, the Keyword field relies on exact matches. Wildcards can help here, as well. (`Regiment` will find different collections than `Regiments`; `Regiment*` will find both)

## FILTERING THE COLLECTIONS

Just like the Search Results page, you can filter the Card Catalog by Category. Unlike the Search Results page, you can also filter by Location, Date, and Language. Filters that you have applied are displayed and may be cleared by clicking the X next to them. In the example below, the collections are filtered to Census & Voter Lists in Canada from the 1800s which are in French. Currently, there are 3 such collections.

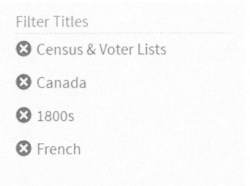

Simply click on one of the Categories, Dates, Locations, or Languages to filter. Some filters have sub-filters: Birth, Marriage & Death is a broad filter, but you can further filter by Birth, Baptism & Christening.

If you get a large set of filters and want to clear everything at once, use the Clear All link above the filters:

## Special Note for Country-Specific Sites

If you are on Ancestry.co.uk or Ancestry.ca or one of the other country-specific Ancestry sites, the Card Catalog is pre-filtered to only show collections from that country. If you want to see other collections, you need to clear the checkbox that appears above the Category filters:

# PART 4: ADVANCED SEARCH TIPS

# ADVANCED SEARCH TIPS

If you are comfortable with the general search options and are ready to dig a bit deeper, this section is for you. These are the tips and tricks gleaned from over six years of working with Search at Ancestry, answering questions and tweaking the system to make improvements where we could. And some are just lesser-known suggestions for making your search experience more productive. Hope you enjoy!

## GLOBAL SEARCH ISN'T REALLY GLOBAL SEARCH

When you start your search from the home page (***www.ancestry.com***) or from the search page (***http://search.ancestry.com*** or ***http://www.ancestry.com/search***), we call this a global search. The idea is that you are searching all of the content hosted by Ancestry.

The truth is, you are not. You are searching *most* of the content, but not all. Allow me to explain.

There is a set of content that Ancestry is not allowed to include in Global search. The only way to search these collections is to go directly to the collection page. Some require that you accept additional terms and conditions before using. Examples of this include the *Nova Scotia, Canada Deaths, Marriages, and Births* collections. (This reinforces the tip to use the Card Catalog to find specific collections for the locations you are searching in.)

There are also collections that are not indexed. Only the images are available. You can browse through them, but you can't search them. How do you find them? Through the Card Catalog. Most are in the Stories, Memories & Histories category. One delightful find is "The Book of Household Management." You won't find many names, but you will find some insights on the time period (1869). You will know when you have found one when the collection-specific search page doesn't have a search form. There are several of these collections, so I do not include a complete list here. Perhaps I can provide it as a separate guide or blog post at a later date.

There are also collections that are not fully indexed. The collections making up the US Probates are probably the largest set. In this set are many images without an indexed entry, and there are wills without an indexed entry. Due to the size of that collection set, the ongoing indexing remains a work in progress. Keep checking back; in the interim, being willing to explore and browse the images in the image viewer can help you make discoveries.

Finally, and this is the big one, a Global search doesn't directly return results from Member Trees, public or private. Trees are indexed, but they are generally not included in the primary search results. You can use the Categories drilldown to view results from trees, or you can use the Categories view on the results page to open the Public or Private Member Trees collections, but the Records view in the Search Results does not display results from the tree collections. *(Yes, there are cases when a matching person from a family tree will show up at the top, but this is an exception rather than a rule.)*

As a sub-category to this topic, if you are using an Ancestry Institutions or Ancestry Library account in your public library, or if you have one of the LDS Subscriptions, then a global search may be even more restricted. Due to contractual arrangements with some of the content providers, not all collections are allowed to be used with these subscriptions. Ancestry has a policy of not making the list of these collections public, and I will respect their policy (there are some blogs with partial lists, if you are interested). But it is something you should be aware of. A personal Ancestry World Subscription provides the most complete access to the Ancestry collection set.

## Exact = Required

This is a simple concept, but it is one that takes a moment to wrap your head around. Let's look at an example:

> Look for a marriage record for Robert Coats. He lived in Illinois, was born in 1872, and died in 1922. He was probably married in 1895, +/- 5 years. If you fill in these details, mark everything as **Exact** (putting the range on the marriage date), and click Search, you will get 0 results.

When you mark a field as Exact when you do a search, the underlying search engine also flags that field as *Required*. This conflation of capabilities generally makes sense, except when it messes with your results.

What do I mean by required? The collection being searched MUST HAVE the field in it for the collection to be searched. The record in the collection MUST HAVE a value for that field in it for the record to be found.

In this example, looking for Robert Coats, the primary problem is including the Death Date and making it exact:

Remembering that *Exact = Required*, 0 results actually makes sense. Marriages happen between two living people. Birth dates may be mentioned, but – since the bride and groom are alive – no death dates are included. By marking the death date as exact, you are also requiring that field to be in the collection. No marriage collections have death dates, so no results are returned. To correct this, use the slider to pull the Death Year back to broad, or edit the search to de-select the Exact checkbox on the death date, and you will get the results you expected.

This tends to cause more problems when searching from a Tree and "Match all terms exactly" is selected, but it can trip you up as you move in and out of categories.

And for those who jumped ahead to this section to understand why Ancestry does a "not male" or "not female" search when including Gender in the search, here is your answer. Remember that Gender searches are Exact searches. And Exact = Required. If the underlying search did an "exact male," it would only find records where the gender is specified and the gender is male. All other records would be excluded. This way, Ancestry can return promising matches even when the gender is not specified in the record.

## PHRASE SEARCHES

Many search systems support phrase searches, where you put a set of words in quotes. The expectation is that the quote will be found exactly as entered.

However, Ancestry doesn't support phrase searches.

With that said, there are some cases where Ancestry sort of supports phrase searches.

Phrases are partially supported in the Keyword field when you are searching OCR content. But even then, it is not a real phrase – it is more of an ordered proximity search. Put the phrase in quotes – `"north park"` – and mark it as exact. Remember that OCR content is often mangled. Adding wildcards can help you find some of these mangled terms, but you can't use both wildcards and quotes. You may have to try some different combinations to find what you need.

## GIVEN & MIDDLE NAMES

Ever have this happen to you? You look for `Mary Elizabeth Walker`, but Ancestry keeps finding records for `Elizabeth Mary Walker` instead.

Ancestry provides a field for First & Middle Names. While order is important to you, it is not important to the search engine. Mary Elizabeth scores just as high as Elizabeth Mary. Both records will score higher than a record containing only one of the names. Similarly, a record for Mary scores just as high as a record for Elizabeth.

At the moment, there is no workaround for this. Adding quotes doesn't help. You just need to be aware of it and account for it when reviewing results.

# Maiden Names & Married Names

When you are searching for a married woman, do you include the maiden name, the married name, or both?

The correct answer for this goes back to your primary search strategy: What is it that you are trying to find?

If you are looking for the woman after she was married, then search for her married name. Alternately, if she is younger, search for her maiden name. This will help you avoid extra records that do not apply.

As a special note, when searching from a woman in your tree, the search automatically includes both the maiden name and married name (if both are available). For example, Mary Wilson married George W Scott. A search from Mary in the tree will search for Mary Wilson Scott.

Using this example, the first record returned is for Mary Wilson, married to George B Wilson. The match on the maiden name brings back the wrong information:

| | |
|---|---|
| 1900 United States Federal Census<br>CENSUS & VOTER LISTS<br><br>View Image | NAME: **Mary Wilson**<br>SPOUSE: George B Wilson<br>OTHER: Georgia<br>[Arthur]<br>BIRTH: May 1872 - Missouri<br>MORE: See all information... |

By editing the search and removing the maiden name, the correct result floats to the top:

| | |
|---|---|
| 1900 United States Federal Census<br>CENSUS & VOTER LISTS<br><br>View Image | NAME: **Mary Scott**<br>SPOUSE: George Scott<br>OTHER: May B<br>BIRTH: Jan 1870 - Missouri<br>MORE: See all information... |

Editing the search to remove the extra name can help focus the results and lead to a greater likelihood of a valid discovery.

# MEXICO & NAME SEARCHES

Ancestry has a growing set of collections from Mexico and Latin America. If you have Latin heritage, and can read Spanish, you may consider using the *http://www.ancestry.mx* site to do your searches. This site splits the surname field into two fields: **Apellido paterno** and **Apellido materno**. While this is convenient, and matches how these names are constructed, *it doesn't change the underlying search.*

The following two searches for Jose Perez Quinones are identical:

| BUSCAR | ☐ Todos los términos deben coincidir de forma exacta | |
|---|---|---|
| **Nombres** | **Apellido paterno** | **Apellido materno** |
| Jose | Perez | Quinones |
| ☐ Exacto… | ☐ Exacto… | |

| SEARCH | ☐ Match all terms exactly |
|---|---|
| **First & Middle Name(s)** | **Last Name** |
| Jose | Perez Quinones |
| ☐ Exact… | ☐ Exact… |

Ancestry doesn't index the paternal or maternal surnames separately. They are both indexed as surnames. Valid results (from the search engine perspective), include

- Jose Perez
- Jose Quinones
- Jose Perez Quinones
- Jose Quinones Perez

Be careful as you search your Latin heritage, as you may find records in the search results that don't belong to your ancestors.

# NEWSPAPERS, BOOKS, AND OTHER OCR COLLECTIONS

Once you get past all of the "easy" collections, like the censuses and birth, marriage, & death collections, you may find yourself in the Newspapers and other collections that have been processed using Optical Character Recognition (OCR) technology. These can be great collections to find information about your ancestors or to learn more about what life was like during the time period your ancestors lived in. However, they are very different to use than the *fielded* collections.

You can recognize, from the search results page, when you are about to view an OCR collection. Rather than the search results showing a summary of the record, you will get an image snippet:

| Results 1–50 of 120,015 | | | | | |
|---|---|---|---|---|---|
| View Image | | State | City | Newspaper | Date |
| *[image snippet]* Showing 3 of 9 matches found on this image. | *[image snippet]* | Texas | Abilene | Abilene Reporter-News, The | 3 Aug 1937 |
| *[image snippet]* Showing 2 of 7 matches found on this image. | *[image snippet]* | Texas | Abilene | Abilene Reporter-News, The | 26 Sep 1937 |

Clicking on the snippet takes you into the Image Viewer, where you can view the full newspaper page or the book page. Your search terms, where possible, are highlighted on the snippet and in the image viewer.

Just because these collections are different doesn't mean they are bad or of less value. Some of my best discoveries have come from newspapers and books. You just have to think about them a bit differently. To start with, you need to understand how OCR indexing works.

For the main Ancestry collections, like a census, each fact is read by a human and keyed into a program. That program associates the fact with a field, such as First Name, Last Name, Birth Date, or Birth Location. These fields are then indexed for searching. These are fielded collections. If the information is not keyed into the program, it is not searchable.

With an OCR collection, the information is scanned and read by a computer. The computer looks at the text on the page of the newspaper or book and attempts to understand the letters and words on the page. Those words, as identified by the computer, are indexed. There are no fields. Each page is essentially a big list of words. The index knows which pages has which words, and it knows where on the page those words are (which allows Ancestry to highlight your search terms). But the index doesn't know if the word "Baker" is a last name, a job description, a business name, a street name, or a city name.

OCR collections may also have more misspellings in them. Newspapers may be blurry, or the page may have been poorly aligned when it was scanned, or there may have been a wrinkle on the page, or the font used was hard for the computer to recognize. Regardless of the cause, you may need to get creative in how you search these valuable – but sometimes frustrating – collections.

## TIPS FOR SEARCHING NEWSPAPERS, BOOKS, AND OTHER OCR COLLECTIONS

- Use Exact. This forces the word to appear in the index.
- Use Name variants as needed.
- Use Wildcards as needed.
- The search engine does try to account for names. If you have a first and last name, it gives a higher score to documents where the first and last name are closer together.
- For all other search terms, they only need to occur somewhere in the document (or be related to the publication place).
- The Keywords field gives you a small amount of additional control. You can put other related terms into the Keywords field when searching Newspapers and Books. Using Exact can help you find more relevant newspapers. (See *Effective Use of the Keyword Field* for additional tips.)

# UNDERSTANDING LIFESPAN FILTERING

Ancestry does some useful things with dates. If you understand what is going on, you can gain greater control over your search and understand why some records are returned and some are filtered out.

In order to make the search engine more efficient, whenever you search using a date, Ancestry pre-filters some records out of the results. Ancestry makes an assumption of how long a person may have lived, based on the dates you provide. If you give a birth and death date, then the lifespan for the person is fairly well set. Ancestry will pad the stated lifespan to catch records that are off by a few years, but since you have provided the general lifespan, that is what is used. Any record that has a date in it and that doesn't fall in the lifespan (plus padding) is excluded.

Conceptually, this should make sense. If your ancestor was born in 1920, you don't need to see records from 1900. If he died in 1930, you don't need to see records from 1940. The filtering makes the search more efficient.

If you don't provide a lifespan – the birth or death date is unknown, then Ancestry has to make some assumptions. If you say a person was born in 1860, then Ancestry automatically filters out people who are born several years before that. A record with a date of 1858 would be returned; a record from 1850 would not. However, a record from 1950 could be returned, as the person could have lived that long. A record from 1990 would not, as that is far outside a typical lifespan. A similar process is used when you only provide a death date.

What about when a person is married? If you only provide a marriage date, can you make any assumptions on when the person was born or when they died? In some cultures, marriages happened very young. Or, a couple could be married when they are very old. The date range for this becomes quite broad.

The broadest lifespan happens with Lived In or Any Event dates. If the search engine only knows that a person lived in or did something in a location in 1850, then that person could have been very young when it happened or very old. The lifespan is very broad and will include more possible records.

The specific values used in lifespan filtering are:

- Birth: -5 years. If you specify a birth year of 1910, the lifespan filter will automatically exclude any records from before 1905.
- Death: +5 years. If you specify a death year of 1910, the lifespan filter will automatically exclude any records from after 1915.
- Birth & Death: -5 years from the stated birth; +5 years from the stated death. If you specify a birth in 1875 and a death in 1955, then all records outside of 1870-1960 are excluded.
- Marriage: The earliest age for a marriage is assumed to be 13 years. The oldest age for a marriage is assumed to be 100 years. If you only provide a marriage date, then the lifespan is assumed to be -87 years and +100 years from the specified date, giving a range of 187 years.
- Military: Follows the same pattern as Marriage events. The earliest age is assumed to be 13, and the old age is assumed to be 100 (not for active duty, but potentially for pensions or awards). -87 years to +100 years.
- Arrival & Departure: -100 years to +100 years from the stated date. Infants and the elderly traveled, so the lifespan is broad.
- Live In or Any: -100 years to +100 years from the stated event. Since these events can capture a huge range of event types, there is no real way to narrow down the range effectively.

If you use the Exact +/- options in your dates, then these ranges are *increased* or *decreased* by the amount you specify.

Now that you know all of this, how does it help you with your searches?

First, it should encourage you to make your searches more precise when you can. Providing dates that you know (in the right context) can help narrow down the results set and help you find the record you are looking for.

Second, it should help you understand the search results you get back. Sometimes, you will find records in the search results that appear to be decades away from what seems "normal" for the person you are searching for. Adding or clarifying dates (even if they are estimates) can help eliminate outliers from the results.

Third, using the **Exact +/-** on dates gives you some additional control over the upper and lower boundaries of the lifespan.

# Understanding Relevancy Ranked Results: Part 3

You understand the basics of relevancy ranking – the more search terms you have that match in the record, the higher the relevancy score. The records with the highest scores are listed first.

Of course, it can't be that easy. And the scoring algorithms are complex. I can't cover the proprietary details, but I can provide some insight.

First, just having a lot of stuff in your search doesn't necessarily mean you will get a truly relevant record. Some pieces of information are more important than others when calculating the score. The *primary name* on the record is the most important; matches on the primary name get the highest score. *Secondary names* are less important; matches on those get a lower score. (A primary name is who the record is about; secondary names are others who are mentioned on a record. For example, in a birth record, the primary name is the child; the secondary names are the parents.)

Second, the name variant options affect the score. Ancestry does fuzzy matching by default. Records which exactly match the name get a higher score than those that match a variant on the name. (If you enter William in the search form, a record with William in it will score higher than a record with Wm or Will.)

Third, Ancestry employs a minimum score. If a record doesn't receive a high enough score, it is dropped from the results. The exception to this is when only a single term is used in the search; with a single term, especially if it is not a surname, there is not enough detail to provide a good score, so all scores are returned. Minimum scores generally don't cause problems, unless you are not searching for a primary name. For example, searching a census for the father's name (in the Father's First Name and Father's Last Name fields) *and nothing else* may return no records, since the minimum score threshold may not be met.

Fourth, if you want to get higher scoring matches, include the Primary Name, one or more dates, and one or more locations. Including an appropriate secondary name helps as a discriminating factor and can give a record a higher score.

Finally, remember that your goal isn't to create the perfect search to return the perfect record. Your goal is to provide enough information to find new information. Usually, you can do this with 4-6 search terms, if you tune the Exact options and either use the Category filters or search specific collections.

As a bonus tip, you should also be aware that Ancestry boosts certain collections in each geography. Usually, these are the most important collections, but they could also be new collections that they want to promote. The boost is minimal and only serves as a tie breaker if all other things are equal. The collections they boost are relatively fixed, but they can change over time.

## CATEGORY EXACT MODE

Hidden in the Site Preferences is a sometimes-helpful Search setting. To find it, click on your name in the upper right corner, then click on Site Preferences.

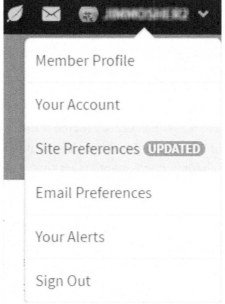

Scroll down the page to the Search Preferences:

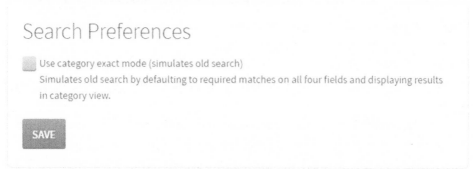

Setting this option does the following:

- Sets the Search Results display to the Categories view rather than the Records view. (You can switch back and forth during your session, but your default setting will be the Categories view.)
- Moves the **Match all terms exactly** option to the top of the Global search form. (This is normally "hidden" under the **Show more options link**.)
- Selects the **Match all terms exactly** option, which can create a more focused search when using limited information.
- Disables the "Person Picker" on the Global search form.
  - If you switch to one of the other search forms, such as the category form for Census & Voter Lists, you can use the Person Picker, but the "Match all terms exactly" will be disabled when the person information is loaded into the form.
- Changes the Global search form to display a year range:

☑ Match all terms exactly

First & Middle Name(s)                                    Last Name

Lived in (state or country)                               Year range
City, County, State, Country                                    to

SEARCH    Show more options ∨    Clear search

The year range looks like it could be useful. This is what people think it does:

> Find all people with the last name of Rogers who lived in Macon County, Georgia, between 1860 and 1880.

That would be a great option. However, it doesn't work that way. Let's take a look at the results for this search, as entered into the search form:

☑ Match all terms exactly

First & Middle Name(s)

Last Name

Rogers

✔ Exact & soundex

Lived in (state or country)

Macon County, Georgia, USA

Year range

1860 to 1880

✔ Exact to this place

The search results (in the Categories view) are:

308 results

RECORDS | CATEGORIES

Census & Voter Lists — 77

1900 United States Federal Census — 17

Georgia, Returns of Qualified Voters and Reconstruction Oath Books, 1867-1869 — 14

1880 United States Federal Census — 13

1930 United States Federal Census — 10

1870 United States Federal Census — 8

See all 77 results...

The date range was clearly for 1860 – 1880. Why are there results in the 1900 and 1930 Censuses? Shouldn't it only return records between 1860 and 1880?

Part of the challenge is in the **Lived In (state or county)** field. Underneath, this is NOT using the Lived In field. It is using the Any Location field. The search is more accurately interpreted as:

> Find everyone with the last name of Rogers who *ever* did anything in Macon County, Georgia between 1860 and 1880.

If Bill Rogers was born in Macon in 1865, then he lived there in the date range. If he later moved and was enumerated in the 1930 Census in California, he will be found by this search, since his birth date and birth location match the criteria.

Should you use this search preference? It really depends on your search practices. I know professional researchers who focus on a relatively small geographic area (one or two states). For them, this form – as shown above – combined with the Categories view, gives them just what they need. *For most users, however, I do not recommend this option.*

I do recommend being aware of and appropriately using the Categories view, as discussed previously.

## CATEGORIES VIEW – MISSING RECORDS

Using the Categories view provides a great overview of the collections that have search results. If you are starting with a Category or Global search, the Categories view can give you a quick summary of the types of collections that could be relevant to your search. It allows you to explore a particular collection more completely, rather than work through the traditional relevancy ranked Records view. Refer to *Seeing Which Collections Have Results – Using the Categories View* for general information on the Categories view.

However, there is an undocumented feature that leads to confusion. It shows up most often in Birth and Marriage records, and it comes from the fact that Ancestry creates "extra" records from these record types.

Let's take a look at an example, show the problem, and then explain what is going on.

Do a search in the **Birth, Marriage & Death** category for Norma Davidson, who lived in Indiana. For this example, we'll mark the name and location as exact.

Search

# Birth, Marriage & Death

View sample images and collection details

**SEARCH**    Match all terms exactly

First & Middle Name(s)

norma

✓ Exact

Last Name

davidson

✓ Exact

| | Day | Month | Year | Location |
|---|---|---|---|---|
| Birth | ▼ | ▼ | | City, County, State, Count |
| Death | ▼ | ▼ | | City, County, State, Count |
| Marriage | ▼ | ▼ | | City, County, State, Count |
| Any Event | —— | —— | | Indiana, USA |

✓ Exact to this place

The results for this search, in the Categories view, shows nine results in the *Indiana, Marriage Certificates, 1958-2005* collection:

| 74 results | | RECORDS | CATEGORIES |
|---|---|---|---|

Sort by name | results count

| | |
|---|---|
| Indiana, Marriages, 1810-2001 | 26 |
| Indiana, Birth Certificates, 1907-1940 | 19 |
| Indiana, Marriage Certificates, 1958-2005 | 9 |
| Web: Marion County, Indiana, Marriage Index, 1925-2012 | 5 |
| Indiana, Select Marriages Index, 1748-1993 | 4 |
| U.S., Social Security Applications and Claims Index, 1936-2007 | 4 |
| U.S., Find A Grave Index, 1600s-Current | 2 |
| Indiana, Marriage Index, 1800-1941 | 2 |
| Indiana, Death Certificates, 1899-2011 | 1 |
| Michigan, Death Records, 1867-1950 | 1 |
| Web: Obituary Daily Times Index, 1995-Current | 1 |

But, when you click on the collection to view the results, you get six, not nine:

Results 1–6 of 6

| View Record | Name | Marriage Date | Marriage City | Spouse | View Images |
|---|---|---|---|---|---|
| View Record | Norma Jean Davidson | 16 Apr 1964 | New Albany | John Dunning Davis | |
| View Record | Norma Joan Davidson | 14 Nov 1988 | Indianapolis | James Donald Henson | |
| View Record | Norma Joan Davidson | 11 Jan 1980 | Indianapolis | James Donald Henson | |
| View Record | Norma Jean Davidson | 13 Jan 1964 | Muncie | Shirley Jamijar | |
| View Record | Norma R. Davidson | 12 Oct 1985 | Indianapolis | Larry E. Lynch | |
| View Record | Norma J. Davidson | | Jeffersonville | Roger W. Cory | |

1–6 of 6                                                                 Per page 50 ▼

We have gone from 9 results to 6 results. Why?

In this case, there are 6 records which list Norma Davidson as the bride. There are 3 records which list Norma Davidson as the mother of the bride. The Categories view lists all of them. The collection-specific search results just list the six.

Getting confused? Let's look at this specific example a little more closely.

The search is for Norma Davidson, who lived in Indiana. We find her in the Indiana Marriages collection. In running this search, Ancestry does the following:

- Looks for records where Norma Davidson is the *primary* person in the record. Records where she is the spouse are considered primary – the record is about her.
- Looks for records where Norma Davidson is a *secondary* person in the record. Records where Norma Davidson is listed as the mother of the bride are considered secondary – the record is *not* about her, but she is listed in the record.

The Categories view counts both the *primary* and *secondary* records. The collection-specific view only counts the *primary* records. That means the Categories view gets all nine results and collection-specific view only get six.

(Keep reading...I explain the why Ancestry does this in a moment.)

If you want to see the "missing" three records, change the search to look for Norma Davidson as the Mother:

**SEARCH**  ☐ Match all terms exactly

| First & Middle Name(s) | Last Name |
|---|---|
|  |  |

|  | Day | Month | Year | Location |
|---|---|---|---|---|
| Birth | — | — |  | City, County, State, Countr |
| Marriage | ▼ | ▼ |  | City, County, State, Countr |
| Any Event | ▼ | ▼ |  | Indiana, USA |

✓ Exact to this place

**Add family member:**  Father  Mother  Spouse  Child

|  | First & Middle Name(s) | Last Name |  |
|---|---|---|---|
| Father |  |  | ✕ |
| Mother | norma | davidson | ✕ |

☑ Exact  ☑ Exact

## The search results will show three results, none of which show Norma:

Results 1–3 of 3

| View Record | Name | Marriage Date | Marriage City | Spouse | View Images |
|---|---|---|---|---|---|
| View Record | Teresa Lynn Davidson | 5 May 2005 | Jeffersonvile | Kevin Guerrero | 🖼 |
| View Record | Sandra Lee Davidson | 27 Jun 1994 | Lafayette | Albert Denton Pickett | 🖼 |
| View Record | George Russell Davidson | 4 Aug 1990 | Evansville | Krista Renee Elpers | 🖼 |

However, if you preview or view these records, you will see Norma Davidson as the mother:

| | |
|---:|:---|
| Name: | Teresa Lynn Davidson |
| Gender: | Female |
| Age: | 55 |
| Birth Year: | abt 1950 |
| Birth Place: | Indiana |
| Marriage Date: | 5 May 2005 |
| Marriage Place: | Jeffersonvile, Clark, Indiana, USA |
| Father: | George C. Davidson |
| Mother: | Norma Davidson |
| Spouse: | Kevin Guerrero |
| Certificate Number: | 011053 |

That explains what is going on and one way to get around it when it happens. The follow up question that I get most often is "Why? Why does Ancestry do this? Why not show everything?" While that is technically three questions, they are usually all asked in the same breath, so I count them as one. And if you really want to know why, read on. Otherwise, skip forward to the next tip.

## WHY ANCESTRY HIDES RECORDS IN THE COLLECTION-SPECIFIC VIEW

The super-short answer is that a filter is applied to the collection-specific search results that is not applied to the Categories view. The filter eliminates the *secondary* records, leaving just the *primary* records.

The longer answer has to do with how the collection-specific search results are displayed. By comparison, when you do a global or category search, you get a summary view of the results. The information displayed in each result varies, as each collection has different types of information. In the example below, you will see that records from three different collections have different types of summary information available:

1920 United States Federal Census
1920S

View Image

NAME: Robert Barham
SPOUSE: Lola Barham
BIRTH: abt 1876 - Missouri
RESIDENCE: 1920 - Blytheville Ward 2,
Mississippi, Arkansas

1881 England Census
1880S

View Image

NAME: Charles Robert Barham
OTHER: John Henry Barham
[James William Barham]
BIRTH: abt 1872 - South Repps, Norfolk,
England
RESIDENCE: 1881 - Southrepps, Norfolk,
England

1891 England Census
1890S

View Image

NAME: Robert Barham
OTHER: William A Barham
BIRTH: abt 1872 - Ashford, Kent, England
RESIDENCE: Ashford, Ashford, Kent

When you drill down into a specific database, the search results are displayed in columns. The columns vary between collections, but for a single collection, the columns are always the same. The columns are selected to show the most useful information in a summary format. The hope is that the search results give you enough information to identify likely candidate records before you actually view the record. In this Indiana Marriage Certificates example, there are four useful columns (with two additional columns for viewing the transcript or viewing the image):

| View Record | Name | Marriage Date | Marriage City | Spouse | View Images |
|---|---|---|---|---|---|

Name, Marriage Date, Marriage City, and Spouse – all good differentiators as you scan the search results, provided the records in the list are about one of the primary people (bride or groom). What happens to the display when it is about a secondary person?

Let's take a look.

We have a record for Norma Joan Davidson, married to James Donald Henson, on 14 Nov 1988, in Indianapolis. Norma's father is Harry R Preusz; her mother is Emma McPheter. James' father is James Hensen Sr; his mother is Barbara C Horsley. When Ancestry creates the primary and secondary records, direct family relationships are also indexed.

Because there are up to six people on the original record, Ancestry creates 6 indexed records:

1. Primary: Groom, married to the Bride, with his father and mother
2. Primary: Bride, married to the Groom, with her father and mother
3. Secondary: Father of the groom, his son, and the son's mother (which may or may not be the father's spouse)
4. Secondary: Mother of the groom, her son, and the son's father (which may or may not be the mother's spouse)
5. Secondary: Father of the bride, his daughter, and the daughter's mother (which may or may not be the father's spouse)
6. Secondary: Mother of the bride, her daughter, and the daughter's father (which may or may not be the mother's spouse)

If we put all of these into a table, with the columns available for display, this is what we get:

| Name | Marriage Date | Marriage City | Spouse |
|---|---|---|---|
| Norma Jean Davidson | 14 Nov 1988 | Indianapolis | James Donald Henson |
| Harry R Preusz | | | |
| Emma McPheter | | | |
| James Donald Henson | 14 Nov 1988 | Indianapolis | Norma Jean Davidson |
| James Hensen, Sr | | | |
| Barbara C Horsley | | | |

Those empty columns don't contain useful information for the secondary records, so the entire row is filtered out. The information that would be in those secondary records are contained in the *primary* records. The assumption is that if you are smart enough to be looking for a marriage or birth record in an individual collection, then you are smart enough to look in the primary records for related family details.

# GOING BEYOND PERSON-BASED SEARCHES

Ancestry has a broad collection of records, some of which are not about people at all. Many are about places. Discovering more about the area your ancestors lived in can be exciting and informative. Use the Card Catalog to explore:

- The Pictures collections. Find a photo of the ship your ancestor traveled on. Explore photos from the Civil War. See postcards from around the world. Or, one of my favorites, see photos from parishes and villages in the UK. (Have an ancestor who was born in a parish in the UK? Chances are, you can find a picture of that parish – search for `Village Photos` in the Card Catalog for this one.)

- The Maps, Atlases, and Gazetteers collections. See how parish boundaries have changed over time. See who owned land before your ancestors settled on it. Explore Civil War battle maps, or check the railroad routes through a particular county or state. If maps don't show the information you are looking for, peak into the Gazetteers, which typically list all of the places in a geographical area, even if they aren't shown on a map (and can help you identify where on the map they belong). These resources provide historical context and are worth exploring.

- A bit less exciting, but still useful, are the Reference, Dictionaries, and Almanacs. Want to know what is in the Library of Congress? There is a resource here to help you.

These resources may not help you grow your tree by adding more people to it, but they can help you tell the story of your ancestors. Understanding the time period they lived in, finding pictures of places they lived or may have visited, help engage you – and your audience – as you share your family history stories.

# SAVING A SEARCH

Ancestry allows you to save records to a Shoebox for future review. Ancestry also saves your most recent searches, in case you want to run them again. But the Shoebox gets messy (there is no way to organize it), and the Recent Searches is a finite list (the search you did last month may not be there; the search you did yesterday might be there). The question is, how do you keep track of searches you may want to repeat, modify, or cite in your research log?

I use Evernote and Wunderlist. Both are free apps (with paid options, if you want some extra capabilities). There are other note-taking and list making applications that would also work. Find the one that works for you. Ideally, find one that allows you to access and add to your notes from any device (your computer or phone or tablet). I have also used the Notes feature on individuals in my family tree on Ancestry. Whatever you choose, here is one strategy for keeping track of your searches:

1. Create a structure in your application for family lines and individuals. You may also want to separate things out by major geographical area as your tree (and notes) grow.

2. When you have done a search, copy the URL from the Search Results page and paste it to your notes or list in the appropriate place. Add a comment about what the search was for. (Don't list all of the search parameters – you just need enough so you can identify it later.)

3. When you need to re-run the search, typically just clicking on the URL in the note application will work. If not, copy the URL and paste it into your browser of choice.

Why should you keep track of the searches you have done? Some reasons are:

- Avoiding repeated searches. If you have already looked in a collection once, do you need to look again? Your notes can help you avoid duplicate work.

- Repeating searches when collections are updated. Some collections at Ancestry are a work-in-progress. New information is added, or existing information is updated. Use the Card Catalog to see which collections have been updated recently and re-run searches that didn't produce results in the past.

- Documenting what you have done. When you share information with others, you should have done a reasonably exhaustive search of the available information. Knowing where you have looked – and where you haven't – can give you confidence that you have done all you can or provide you with ideas for where else you might check.

# CONCLUSION

Family History is an on-going process of discovery. Some discoveries come easy. Some require a bit more work. As you search Ancestry, make the process more effective by remembering the key search strategies:

- Start with what you know
- Clearly identify what you want to know
- Identify where the information is most likely at, and limit your search to that area

Once you have your strategy in place, use the search tips and guidance you have learned from this book to tease out the family history treasures that are just waiting to be found.

# PART 5:
# RECORD COVERAGE, GLOSSARY, & TIP SUMMARIES

# ANCESTRY RECORD COVERAGE

Ancestry adds, on average, over two million new records every day. Their coverage of records from around the world continues to grow. However, there remain areas with little or no coverage. If you aren't finding the records you are looking for, it could be that Ancestry just doesn't have them, hasn't indexed them yet, or doesn't yet have them available on the site. Keep in mind that a search for content that doesn't exist will never return the results you are looking for.

The collection set for Ancestry heavily favors the United States, Canada, and Europe, with most of the European collections being in the United Kingdom and Germany.

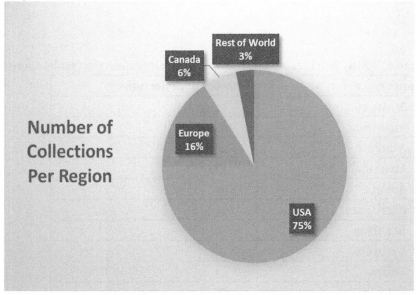

You can gather the same information yourself from the Card Catalog by filtering on the location you are interested in and then referring to the number of collections for that geographical area at the top of the page.

# Card Catalog

Searchable listing of all record collections

| Title | | Collection | Records | Activity |
|---|---|---|---|---|
| Results 1-25 of 295 | | | Sort By Popularity ▼ | |
| Public Member Photos & Scanned Documents | | Pictures | 208,704,547 | |
| British Army WWI Service Records, 1914-1920 | | Military | 3,651,082 | |
| British Army WWI Medal Rolls Index Cards, 1914-1920 | | Military | 5,280,584 | |
| Public Member Stories | | Stories, Memories & Histories | 18,432,579 | |
| British Army WWI Pension Records 1914-1920 | | Military | 2,139,613 | |

**Title**

**Keyword(s)**

SEARCH  or  Clear All

Filter Titles
❌ Europe
❌ United Kingdom
❌ Northern Ireland

The table, below, provides a snapshot of the Ancestry collection set by country.

| Country | Number of Collections |
|---|---|
| Albania | 21 |
| Argentina | 9 |
| Armenia | 22 |
| Australia | 219 |
| Austria | 79 |
| Azerbaijan | 21 |
| Bahamas | 10 |
| Barbados | 12 |
| Belarus | 43 |
| Belgium | 88 |
| Bolivia | 6 |
| Brazil | 24 |
| Bulgaria | 22 |
| Canada | 2010 |
| Chile | 8 |
| Colombia | 7 |
| Costa Rica | 9 |
| Croatia | 30 |

| Country | Number of Collections |
|---|---|
| Czech Republic | 75 |
| Denmark | 54 |
| Dominican Republic | 9 |
| Ecuador | 6 |
| El Salvador | 8 |
| Estonia | 27 |
| Finland | 26 |
| France | 564 |
| Germany | 1914 |
| Ghana | 4 |
| Greece | 25 |
| Grenada | 5 |
| Guatemala | 10 |
| Haiti | 4 |
| Honduras | 8 |
| Hungary | 56 |
| Iceland | 25 |
| India | 20 |
| Indonesia | 5 |
| Ireland | 204 |
| Italy | 162 |
| Jamaica | 14 |
| Japan | 8 |
| Latvia | 38 |
| Liechtenstein | 21 |
| Lithuania | 58 |
| Luxembourg | 28 |
| Mexico | 160 |
| Micronesia | 4 |
| Moldova | 33 |
| Netherlands | 174 |
| New Zealand | 52 |
| Nicaragua | 7 |

| Country | Number of Collections |
|---|---|
| North Korea | 4 |
| Norway | 40 |
| Panama | 11 |
| Paraguay | 6 |
| Peru | 17 |
| Philippines | 13 |
| Poland | 260 |
| Portugal | 30 |
| Romania | 65 |
| Russia | 35 |
| Samoa | 4 |
| Slovakia | 38 |
| Slovenia | 24 |
| South Africa | 37 |
| South Korea | 5 |
| Spain | 57 |
| Sri Lanka | 5 |
| Sweden | 60 |
| Switzerland | 102 |
| Turkey | 24 |
| Ukraine | 47 |
| United Kingdom | 1999 |
| Uruguay | 7 |
| USA | 25440 |
| Venezuela | 5 |
| Yugoslavia | 26 |
| Zimbabwe | 2 |

# GLOSSARY

**Categories** – A grouping of collections, such as all US Federal Censuses, all UK Censuses, or all Marriage & Divorce records. Ancestry has a few dozen primary categories and several hundred secondary categories. Each category has its own search form, with fields that are specific to that category.

**Categories View** – A view on the Search Results page that displays the categories which contain search results, the top collections from those categories, and the number of records that match your search criteria. Useful for quickly scanning the types of collections available for review and for drilling down into the collection-specific search results page for a collection.

**Category Filters** – A set of filters on the Search Results page that allows you to "drill down" into a particular type of search result (such as Census, Birth, Marriage & Death, or Military). Only records from selected category are displayed.

**Category Search** – A search within a group of collections, such as all Census & Voter Lists or all Immigration & Travel. High-level categories are listed under the Search menu. Additional categories are listed on the right side of the Search > All Collections page.

**Collection** – A grouping of records which may be searched individually. For example, the 1911 England Census is a collection.

**Collection Focus** (search form option) – An option to search collections from a specific country or have to do with a particular ethnicity. Found on the bottom of the Global and Category search forms. May be set automatically on country-specific sites (such as www.ancestry.co.uk).

**Collection Type** (search form option) – An option to search a specific type of collection – historical records, family trees, stories, and photos. Used to filter out broad swathes of collections that are not useful to your current search strategy.

**Collection-specific Search** – A search within a single collection of records on Ancestry. Use this to focus on a specific area or time period or record type. For example, if you know your ancestor lived in Indiana all of her life, a search in the Indiana Marriage Index collection may be more efficient than searching the Marriage Category. Most easily accessed from the Card Catalog or the Explore by Location pages.

**Collection-specific Search Results Page** – A columnar listing of search results from a single collection. This is displayed after searching an individual collection, after using the Category Filters to refine your search to a single collection, or using the Categories view on the Search Results page to view a single collection.

**Edit Search** – A link on the Search Results page that lets you edit, or refine, your existing search without having to start over from scratch.

**Exact** – A search filter that may be applied to most names, dates, and places in your search. Setting the exact filter requires that the search term (or an acceptable variant of it) be found in the record.

**Global Search** – A search of almost all collections on Ancestry (there are some excluded collections). Use this as a starting point for a broad search, and then use the Category Filters or Categories View to focus on a particular topic.

**List of Records** (search results page) – The primary focus of the Search Results Page is the list of records which match your search criteria. The list of records is sorted, with the best matches listed first.

**Messaging System** – An Ancestry feature for communicating with other Ancestry members without needing to share a public email address.

**Person Picker** – A way to pre-fill a search form based on information about a person in your tree. As you start to type a first name in a search form, Ancestry will check for matching names from your active tree. If you pick a person from this list, the fields in the form will automatically fill in. (If you don't want to pick a person, just keep typing and the information manually.)

**Person-based Search** – A search that is based on a person in one of your trees on Ancestry. You can search from the Tree Viewer, the Profile Page, or from a search form. When you do a person-based search, the details from your tree are used to fill in the search. It also enables the Smart Filtering feature.

**Place Picker** – The prompt in Location fields for you to "pick a place" that is known to the Ancestry search system. Selecting from this list enables the Exact filtering options on the place, giving you greater control over your search.

**Primary Name / Primary Person** – The person the record is about. In a birth record, the primary person is the child. In a census record, the primary person is the one in the Name column. In a marriage record, there are two primary people – the bride and groom. Anyone else included on the record is considered a secondary person.

**Record** – (1) A document. (2) A transcription of the information for individuals listed on the document.

**Record Hover** – A preview of the record information that appears on the Search Results Page when you hover the cursor over the link to the full record.

**Records View** – A view on the search results page that displays the results in relevancy ranked order (the best matches to your search are displayed at the top).

**Required** – If a search term is marked as exact, then the underlying field is required to be in a collection for results to be displayed from that collection.

**Search Criteria** – The names, dates, locations, or other terms, and the options associated with them, that comprise your search.

**Search Results Page** – The page that displays the search results for Global and Category searches. Collection names are listed on the left; summary information from each result is listed on the right. Compare with Collection-specific search results page.

**Search Results View** – The way you choose to list the results on the Search Results Page. The default option is the Records view. You may change to the Categories view. Making the change is "sticky," meaning your choice will be remembered.

**Secondary Name / Secondary Person** – A person listed on a record, but is not who the record is about. Parents on a birth record, parents on a marriage record, or siblings in an obituary are all considered to be secondary.

**Sliders** (search results page) – A feature on the search results page for controlling how broadly or narrowly the search engine evaluates names, dates, and locations. Slide to the left to make a search more broad (find more records) and to the right to make it more narrow (find fewer records).

**Smart Filter** – A feature on the search results page that shows the records which are already attached to a person in your tree and which filters out other records from the same collection. Only filters records from collections where each person is believed to only appear once. Only appears on Person-based Searches.

**Sub-categories** – A grouping of related collections which are a subset of a bigger category. For example, Marriage & Divorce collections are a sub-category of Birth, Marriage, & Death collections. The Canadian Census Collection is a sub-category of the Census & Voter Lists category.

**Tree Viewer** – The primary view of your tree on Ancestry. From the tree view, you can navigate through your family tree in either a family view or pedigree view. Clicking a person in the tree viewer allows you to view the profile for that person, search for that person in the Ancestry records, or do a quick edit on that person.

**Tree-based Search** – Variant of Person-based search (see above).

# SUMMARY OF THE TIPS & TRICKS

This is the short version of the book. Refer to it for a quick refresher.

## FOLLOW A SEARCH STRATEGY

1. What do you already know?
2. What do you want to know?
3. Where is that information best found?

## EXPLORING ANCESTRY FOR FREE

4. Visit ***http://search.ancestry.com/search/group/freeindexacom*** to search over 800 free collections on Ancestry
5. Watch for free promotions. Ancestry will often make some collections free for a limited period of time around key events and holidays. Watch your email for details.
6. Use a free trial. Two weeks free can be a great start. Cancel before the two weeks are up to avoid any credit card charges.
7. Explore search results without a subscription. Careful searches can help you deduce facts about your ancestors.

## GENERAL SEARCH TIPS

8. Explore records for the stories they contain. Those stories may be different than family lore, but can still be exciting.
9. Use the expanded Global search form (click **Show more options**).
10. Use the Category Filters to focus on specific record types. These are on the left side of the search results page.
11. Use the Collection Focus to restrict results to a specific geographical area or ethnicity. This appears at the bottom of the Global and Category search forms and beneath the sliders on the search results page.

12. Include the right details in your search. A name, place, and year can help focus your search and make the overall haystack smaller.

13. Estimate birth years of ancestors by counting generations. Add 20 years for each generation.

14. Use the Exact options to narrow your search. See the *Exact Search Tips*, below, for details.

15. Use the Place Picker when entering locations. Use the Exact filters to control the granularity of the search.

16. Be aware of what is indexed in the collection. The US Census collections identify which state or country a person was born in, but not what city or county. If you search for a birth city and mark it as exact, you won't find any US Census records. Alternately, the UK Census collections generally do record the birth city. Read the descriptions at the bottoms of the search forms.

17. Start a search from a person in your tree – and then edit the search as necessary.

18. Case doesn't matter in your search terms. Adam = adam = adaM.

19. Use the shortcut keys on the search results page. n = New Search, r = refine (or edit) search, p = Preview current record, > = Highlight next record, < = highlight previous record.

20. Use multiple tabs to review promising collections or records. Press CTRL and then click (CTRL+Click) on a link to open the collection or page in a new tab.

21. Check other people's trees...but do so with a grain of salt (in some cases, with a tablespoon of salt). These can be good pointers, but not all trees are grown with equal amounts of care.

# Intermediate Search Tips

22. Use the Keyword field in the search form to find street names, parish names, or other descriptive information in the record. Use it when searching newspapers, family histories, or other OCR collections to find business names, historical events, or other details.

23. Use specific events rather than the Lived In or Any events, unless you aren't finding what you need with the specific events. (Lived In and Any events are very broad.)

24. Be aware of alternate names when reviewing search results. The results may not show the alternate names, which can make the results look like they don't apply. Use the record hover or click through to see what other names might be indexed as part of the record.

25. Use the Categories view on the search results page. Switch between the Categories and Records views.

26. Sort the Categories view alpha-numerically or by record count (when you are in a single category).

27. Use Wildcards to help with mangled names. The * matches 0 or more characters. The ? matches a single character. You can use both wildcards in the same search term. You must have at least 3 non-wildcard characters in each search term. The first character in a search term cannot be a wildcard.

28. Make your exact searches fuzzy. Use the Exact options in the search form, the sliders on the search results page, and use wildcards with the Exact options on names or in the keyword field.

29. Use Gender and Race/Nationality with care. You may not get the results you are expecting.

30. When searching from a person in your tree, edit the Places to enable the place filtering.

31. Take advantage of Smart Filtering by searching from a person in your tree.

32. Use the Explore by Location feature to discover collections that are about a specific place. Consider using this feature from one of the country-

specific sites (like ***www.ancestry.co.uk***) to get a more interactive version of the feature.

33. Use the Visit our other sites menu at the bottom of most pages to switch to country-specific site.

34. Use the Card Catalog to find specific collections to search. Use the Category filters. Sort the list by Date Updated.

35. In the Card Catalog, remember that the Title and Keyword search options help you search for collections, not for people in the collections. The Title and Keyword search are also very simple; they match your search criteria exactly (marriage does not find marriages). You can use wildcards in these fields.

36. Once you find a collection in the Explore by Location or Card Catalog, click to view the Collection-specific search form.

## ADVANCED SEARCH TIPS

37. Global search is not really global. It searches most collections, but not all.

38. The Ancestry Library/Institution editions and the LDS Subscription have a subset of the content available in the Ancestry World Explorer subscription. This is due to contract restrictions.

39. Some collections aren't fully indexed. You may need to go "old school" and browse through images to find what you need.

40. Remember that Exact = Required. Setting too many options to Exact can filter out all results.

41. Phrase searches. They don't work on Ancestry. Except they sort of do in the Keyword field when searching newspapers and similar OCR content.

42. Ancestry doesn't distinguish between first and middle names, or between maiden and married names, or multiple last names. If you put two names in a name field, then if either of those names are found, the record is considered a match. Mary Elizabeth Walker ranks the same as Elizabeth Mary Walker.

43. Search newspapers and other OCR collections to find the rare gems. It isn't easy, but there are some tips to help out.

44. Use Lifespan filtering to your advantage. Or, at least understand it so the results returned from your date-based searches make sense.

45. Understand how relevancy works. Primary names are more important than secondary names. Exact matches rank higher than fuzzy matches. Locations and dates are important. Craft an effective search, not a perfect search.

46. Category Exact Mode can be a useful search preference. Some users love it and use it exclusively. For most users, I don't recommend it.

47. Moving from the Categories view into a collection-specific view can cause some records to "disappear." Secondary names are counted in the Categories view, but are filtered out of the collection-specific search results.

48. Ancestry has great collections that don't contain names of people. Explore the pictures, maps, gazetteers, and reference material for other great finds.

49. Ancestry doesn't provide a good way to save a search. Use free apps like Evernote to keep track of the searches you do and that you want to repeat at a later date.

50. Ancestry doesn't have all of the content in the world. You may need to branch out to find other sources of information.

# Exact Search Tips

| | |
|---|---|
| Match all terms exactly | In general, just say no. This can exclude more records than intended. For very carefully crafted searches, this can be effective, but usually is not a good idea |
| Exact + Wildcards | Finds records that match one of the term variants, as controlled by the wildcard. For example, an Exact search for a Ship Name **Luc**\* in the New York Passenger List would find records that match ships named Lucy, Lucania, and Luckenbach. Records without a matching ship name are excluded |
| Exact + Name Variants | Finds records that match one or more of the name variants – such as initials, names that sound similar, names that have similar meanings, or common variants (William and Will, for example) |
| Exact + Date Ranges | Use the +/- on dates to give some wiggle room on the records. Ages were often self-reported or approximated; those ages are used to calculate approximate birth years |
| Exact + Place Variants | When entering a location, Ancestry will provide a list of places that match. PICK ONE OF THE SUGGESTIONS. It makes the search more efficient and gives you more options on the places to be searched |
| Exact + Multiple Terms | If you do an exact search for Mary Elizabeth, you may get records for Elizabeth Mary |
| Exact = Required | An Exact search also means the record MUST have a matching value in the record. Don't add exact death dates when searching for census records. Don't add exact marriage dates when looking for birth records |

# Productivity Tips

| Use Multiple Tabs | CTRL+Click is your friend |
|---|---|
| Use the Country-specific Ancestry sites | If you are researching UK records, go to the Ancestry.co.uk site. If you are researching German records, go to the Ancestry.de site. All of the sites are available from the bottom right corner of most pages (down in the footer). |
| Use Explore by Location | Discover collections that have information for a specific geographic region you are interested in. Located *below* the global search form. |
| Use Explore by Location on one of the Country-specific Ancestry Sites | The Explore by Location map on the country-specific sites is more interactive and more complete than the map on the Ancestry.com site. |

# Card Catalog Tips

| Sort the Collection List | Use the Sort By option to view recently added or updated collections, or to view collections alphabetically. |
|---|---|
| Title Search – Exact Match | This is an EXACT match search. A Title search for "Marriage" find collection titles that contain Marriage. It will NOT find titles that contain "Marriages." |
| Title Search - Wildcards | You can use wildcards to get around this – search for Marriage* to get both Marriage and Marriages. The ? wildcard is also supported. |
| Title Search – Multiple Terms | If you put more than one word into the Title field, then both terms must appear in the title. Order is not important. (Adding quotation marks is not supported – they are ignored.) |
| Keyword Search | Searches the description for the collection. This also an exact search. Wildcards are allowed. |

# DISCLAIMER

This book is not sponsored by, or in any way endorsed by, Ancestry, its parent companies, or its affiliates.

The Ancestry web site is constantly evolving and content is constantly being added. Individual screens may appear differently from what appears in this book, and search results may also be different. However, the concepts presented should still apply.

Most screen captures are taken from the www.ancestry.com site. Other co-branded sites, like www.ancestry.co.uk, are similar.

# About the Author

Jim Mosher worked at Ancestry for over six years. During that time, he worked on Search, the Image Viewer, the Probates experience, and several other projects. He has a broad range of knowledge on the Ancestry feature set. As an avid amateur genealogist, he enjoys learning the stories of his forebears. When he is not writing or researching, Jim enjoys time with his living family, photography, running, hiking, golfing, and the occasional game of racquetball.

Feel free to contact Jim at *JimMosherInsiderSecrets@gmail.com*. Your feedback, success stories, and questions are always appreciated.

Made in United States
North Haven, CT
30 July 2022

22034728R00082